RahGor Reviews

"Rahfeal is pulling the human race forward! The most inspiring leaders are committed to follow a transcendental vision. Becoming a global leader is a never ending journey that constantly pushes individuals to be their best self. Rahfeal is definitely leading by example, establishing the highest standards for himself, while sharing with his peers the wisdom that he is practicing in his own life and business."

—MIGUEL DIAS, FOUNDER AND CEO AT CEO WORLD (PORTO, PORTUGAL)

"Rahfeal and I met as co-speakers at an event in Norway in 2014. Although we live half the world apart, we have been interacting ever since and I do feel happy and at peace writing about him. There are 3 things that I find truly remarkable about Rahfeal. Not all can overcome life situations by just focusing on his strengths—Rahfeal is a fine example. Next is his positivity; to some tepid audience responses Rahfeal would go, 'Awesome!' promptly bringing back life to the discussion. And finally, his humility that radiates calmness and happiness, inspiring many of his friends and followers. Rahfeal is a natural leader and this book is a good reflection of his beliefs. Keep it going, bro!"

—PARTHASARATHY, ENTREPRENEUR, FOUNDER AND CEO AT CADD CENTRE, ISOLVE, IKIX 3D PRINTS, (CHENNAI, INDIA)

"Rahfeal's philosophy of the 3D's, dedication, discipline and determination has inspired many of our students to push forward to reach their personal greatness. His message of light and love truly inspires one to give and be their best."

—**Sandy Marks**, MS & HS Principal, Colegio San Patricio, (Monterrey, Mexico)

"When I hear Rah say to young people 'your location is not your destination,' I see the change start on their faces, and by the time Rah's talk is done it's clear that he has truly affected his audience. Rah has an uncanny ability to connect with young people and help them understand that they can do anything they want in life."

—**Shawn K. Osborne,** President and CEO, NFTE (Network for Teaching Entrepreneurship) (USA)

"RahGor is again inspiring leaders of today and tomorrow all over the World with his new book about leadership. He is illustrating in a very clear way the characteristics of a true and effective leader and the importance of a transcending leadership and humanity. This book can be red over and over again and is a reminder that good leaders never stop learning."

—**Camilla Andersson**, Founder of SparkUp Norge (Bergen, Norway)

"Rahfeal Gordon will touch your life and impact the lives of those who meet him. He encourages people to become better by teaching them the love of life, the value life brings to oneself, their community, and society at large."

—**Roger Leon**, Assistant Superintendent of Administration for Newark Public Schools (USA)

"Given today's modern economy and fast changing cultural dynamics, becoming a global business leader is more challenging than ever. Success requires both the mindset and strategies embodied by Rahfael Gordon. He has generously pulled back the curtain to reveal the specific tools and tactics that he and and other successful international leaders use to inspire, build community and create massive global impact."

—**Ryan Foland**, Managing Partner of InfluenceTree (USA)

"Rahfeal is one of those people whose life experiences are as powerful as his presence. When Rahfeal writes, he means it. The work in this book is an essential blueprint for anyone looking to understand and build the audience for effective leadership."

—**Sachin Narode**, Founder of Xeniapp Inc. & Survive and Thrive (USA)

"This book will change the way leaders think about themselves. I am sure that this book will help our world see more leaders than anyone has even seen in the entire history. If you read this book, you are already on the path of redefining yourself as a great leader."

—**Nishant Manchanda** (India)

"Filled with intriguing stories that will make you want to read more. All of the key values a future Global Leader needs to keep in mind are in *Leading Without Limits*. Your leading practices will be fundamentally doubted. It will make leaders reflect upon what their true objective is. Such easy analogies put in the correct place to explain the situation a leader is in."

—**Diego Elizondo Guzmán**, Co-Founder and President of Grupo Empredil (Chile)

"RahGor is a true inspirator and motivator. Warm and honest. His passion and positivity radiates by ways of how he pours and delivers his thought in the book. Reading *Leading Without Limits* helped me dig deeper and reflect on myself and what I have been doing and achieved as a leader during this past 21 years. Through this book, RahGor has provided us, as leaders, the more practical guide to becoming a better one in leading our squad. Thank you for sharing and igniting us to become a better leader for the humankind."

—**Shinta Witoyo Dhanuwardoyo**, CEO/Founder of Bubu.com, Angel investor and mentor to Startups (Jakarta, Indonesia)

"Mr Rahfeal Gordon' An exceptional Global leadership ambassador, with his new book 'Leading Without Limits' aims to build great leaders around the globe. *Leading Without Limits* is a driving force behind good leadership, and an invaluable performance multiplier for young leaders. Mr. Rahfeal Gordon expertly will empower you to see the leader in you. Well done!"

—**Istar Nur Ahmed**, Youth National Advisor to the Prime Minister, Federal Republic of Somalia

"Rahfeal is a worldwide leader who inspires by action, acumen and kindness. I see Rah working harder and smarter than any other CEO, from leading events at Carnegie Hall to humbly outworking his fellow man. Rah compels you to raise your level of business growth, personal development and community outreach."

—**Seth Kean**, CEO at ROI Influencer Media (USA)

"As an Ambassador, I am always in search of new and better ways to communicate and understand the diverse cultures of men, women, and children I cross paths with. What I have found most notable about Rahfeal is his ability to relate and touch the hearts of all who read his books and hear his message. Not only does he talk the talk, he embodies it in daily action. This timeless book is sure to inspire many young men and women, as it has myself, to realize our full potential and lead the way with authenticity and confidence."

—**Nomi Ganbold**, Ambassador For Women's Empowerment and Peace, International Human Rights Commission & Director of Mongolia EBS, Inc. (USA/Mongolia)

"My dear friends, I have the opportunity to meet Mr. Rahfeal Gordon, in Oslo and from the beginning I understand that he is already a great leader with a tremendous potential. I recently read his book, 'Leading Without Limits' and I discovered an impressive tool for both politicians and businessmen. In his book, Rahfeal reminds us that in any project, we must use freedom and liberty as the foundation stone, because that is the only way to build something that stands in time. Also, this book reminds us that a true leader will appear only in a free and competitiveness world. The book is also teaching us that leadership is about helping and guiding and not about calling the tune. I will surely promote this book among my colleagues."

—**Pavel Popescu**, Member of Romanian Parliament (Romania)

"His insight is truly global and transcends any cultural boundaries. Rahfeal brings to the table ageless wisdom but still talks straight to the new generation of global leaders. He is refreshingly authentic and heartwarming in his leadership style."

—**Sukhvinder Singh Jhotti**, CEO of Scandinavian Health System (Norway)

"Rahfeal has a unique way of getting you galvanized into action around leadership principles that are familiar. For those looking to leverage their current leadership position in the global market, get ready, get ready, get ready."

—**Victoria Pratt**, former Judge, current Law School Professor (USA)

LEADING
WITHOUT LIMITS

A GUIDE TO BECOMING A GLOBAL LEADER

RAHFEAL GORDON

RahGor Publishing & Co.

Copyright © 2018 Rahfeal C. Gordon

All rights reserved. No part of this book may be reproduced, stored, or transmitted by any means—whether auditory, graphic, mechanical, or electronic—without written permission of both publisher and author, except in the case of brief excerpts used in critical articles and reviews. Unauthorized reproduction of any part of this work is illegal and is punishable by law.

ISBN: 978-0-9978311-9-1 (Soft Cover)
ISBN: 978-0-9978311-7-7 (Hard Cover)

Printed in the U.S.A.

"Sometimes it's the people who no one imagines anything of who do the things that no one can imagine."

—THE IMITATION GAME

Contents

1 Raising the Bar on Leadership   1
   The History of Leadership   3
   Chosen vs. Self-Proclaimed Leadership   4
   Chosen Leadership   5
   Self-Proclaimed Leadership   5
   Comparing Leadership Results   7
   Enhancing and Empowering Humanity   8
   Heavy Is the Head That Wears the Crown   11

2 Transcending Leadership   15
   Transcending with Authenticity   17
   Transcending with Humility   18
   Transcending with Transparency   19

3 RahGor's 8 Principles for Leading with Humility   23
   Principle #1: You Don't Know Everything   23
   Principle #2: You're Not the Only One   24
   Principle #3: Don't Fall Victim to Praise   24
   Principle #4: Always Serve Others   24
   Principle #5: Listen More; Speak Less   25
   Principle #6: Question with Passion and Enthusiasm   25

Principle #7: The Community Chose You   26
Principle #8: Be a Student of Life   26

4   The (3) Commitments of a Leader   27

The Wealth of Effective Leadership   27
Commitment #1: Value the people you lead   30
Commitment #2: Relate to the value of others   31
Commitment #3: Enhance the value of others   31

5   The Servant Entrepreneur   35

7 Pillars of a Servant Entrepreneur   37

6   Establishing and Nurturing a Culture of Success   39

Vision and Message of Your Culture   40
Your Team, Your Culture   41
Pay Attention to the Details of Work Ethic   42
A Past Culture of Success   43
RahGor List for a Culture of Success   45

7   The Great Power of Ten   53

1. The Power in Purpose   54
2. The Power in Self Confidence   55
3. The Power in Enthusiasm   55
4. The Power in Expertise   56
5. The Power in Preparation   57
6. The Power in Self-Reliance   58
7. The Power in Image   59

8. The Power of Character   60
9. The Power of Self-Discipline   61
10. The Power in Developing Extraordinary Performance   62
The Gardener's Badge Story   63

8 Measuring Your Impact   67

How to Measure Your Impact   68
Measurement #1: Perception of Leadership   68
Measurement #2: Team Performance   69
Measurement #3: Growth in Following   69
Measurement #4: Set Milestones   70
Measurement #5: Enhancement in Attitude and Behavior   70
Measurement #6: Formation of Relationships   71
Measurement #7: Enhancement in Opportunities   71
Measurement #8: Spark in Innovation   72
Measurement #9: Enhancement in Organizational Structure and Function   72
Measurement #10: Increased Collaboration   73
Measurement #11: Duplication of Leadership Style and Brand   73
Leveraging Your Impact   74
How RahGor Measures Impact   75
The Bell Teacher   76

9 Who Will Save the Super Heroes?   79

10 The Trials and Tribulations of Leadership   81
The Body   81
The Mind   82
The Spirit   84
The Relationships   85
Learning to Move Forward from Failure   87

11 The Reinvention of Yourself   91
Be Honest with You about You   92
Create a Support System   93
Visualize the End First   94
Radical Change Takes Radical Faith   95
Let Truth Settle In   97

12 Mastering Leadership at the Highest Level   99
Always Be Like a Child and Stay Curious   100
Use Your Imagination in its Entirety   100
Never Seek Comfort   101
Let Your Work Speak for You   101
Have a Sense of Purpose   102
Commit to Apprenticeship   102
The Five Steps to Mastery   103
Step One: Discover Your Calling   103
Step Two: Apprentice with Intensity   104
Step Three: Gain Social Intelligence   105
Step Four: Awaken Creative Energy   106

Step Five: Develop High–Level Intuition 107
Abandon Yourself 108

13 Travel the World Constantly 109
Question and Assuming 110
The Road Is Always Under Construction 111
Steering with Your Gut 112
Change of Pace 114

14 Leading Through Engagement 117
Local Community Engagement 118
Global Community Engagement 119
Leadership Team Engagement 120
Inspire Fellow Leaders to Greatness 121

15 The Leadership of Mandela 125
The Answers Are Hidden in the Youth 127
Mandela's Optimism 128
Mandela's Leadership 129
Mandela's Thoughts on Society 131
Mandela and Perseverance 132
Mandela on Peace 133
Mandela on Hate and Love 134

16 The Mindset of Elon 137
Risk the Odds 138
Purpose-Driven Business Leader 139
Talent Beats Numbers 140

Take Advantage of Your Opportunities   141
Aim to Always Do Better   142
Invest in Yourself and Your Dreams   142
Prepare for the Best   144

17   The Opportunity of Having the Privilege   147

18   Handle Your Habits   151
4 Ways To Handle Your Bad Habits   152

19   Strategic Leadership   155
Authoritarian Style   156
Paternalistic Style   156
Democratic Style   157
Laissez-Faire Style   158
Transactional Style   158
Strive for Growth Through Strategic Leadership   159
Change Management   160
The Need for Change Management and Models   161
John Kotter's Eight-Step Process for Leading Change   163

20   Balancing the Change Process   171
Strategic Leadership Process   173
The Execution   173

Leaders and Their Vocabulary 174
Raise the Level of Leadership 175
Get Rid of THEY and Stick with WE 177

❁

A university professor went to visit a famous Zen master to inquire about how he acquired wisdom. While the master served tea, the professor excitedly talked about Zen. The master quietly poured the visitor's cup to the brim, and then continued to pour. The professor watched the overflowing cup until he could no longer restrain himself. He blurted out, "It's too full! No more will go in!"

"You are like this cup," the master replied. "I can only show you Zen when you first empty your cup."

CHAPTER 1

Raising the Bar on Leadership

Leadership: a term that receives so much time in the spotlight. Men and women from all over the world study it, search for it, emulate it, and try to claim it. But leadership—that is, true leadership—is the product of clear vision, action, and a combined list of characteristics that formulate a dynamic individual. This person can help others reach mountaintops, cross seas, fly among the clouds, and see our planet Earth from a distance.

The purpose of this book is to highlight aspects of and go in-depth about the crown of LEADERSHIP. I am not aiming to simply help you be a leader. My ultimate goal is to provide you with the tools to be a *dynamic* leader—an exceptional and extraordinary leader. A leader whose name will create a legacy.

It is essential that current leaders assist in the development of other potential leaders. Leaders' knowledge must continue to flow through this universe. With that said, it is the current leaders' responsibility to sift through the potentials in order to make an informed decision about who to pour that knowledge into, looking at track records and a person's ability to lead in this generation and the generations to come.

Whether locally, nationally, or globally, we need powerful, monumental, earth-shaking, heartbeat-skipping, superhero-like leadership. The world cannot survive on anything less. That is exactly what I want to give you in this book: empowerment that will help you raise the bar on leadership. I want you to be iconic and dynamic in your leadership position.

But leadership is not for the faint of heart. Even with advising you and giving you the powerful tools necessary to maneuver leadership, ultimately, you have to put in the work. This book is for the individuals who show up before the rest of the team to exemplify their respect for the importance of time management. This book is for the individuals who stand in the crowd cheering because they know that leadership isn't always about standing in front. This book is for leaders all over the world who own, manage, and create businesses and organizations to help humanity to thrive and who are still working to learn more.

I created this book so that you can rise to the next level and stand in your greatness by being the extraordinary leader you were called to be.

The History of Leadership

Wisdom gained from applied knowledge teaches that all things deserve to be researched before being obtained. This applies to more than just our beliefs and what we stand for. It is also relevant to the weight we place on titles, as well as the people we encounter in business and personal relationships. Researching and getting acquainted with something or someone are always smart moves for those who seek longevity in their corresponding areas of interest. A few questions you need to ask yourself before we dig any deeper are:

★ Do you truly know what leadership is?

★ Who taught you about leadership?

★ Where did you receive your knowledge about such a high title and position as leadership?

Leadership is defined as *both a research area and a practical skill, regarding the ability of an individual or organization to "lead" or guide other individuals, teams, or entire organizations.* Depending on where you are in the world, you will hear various definitions and viewpoints on this topic. But aside from the differences in language, religion, skin color, and origin, what's truly universal in all leaders are their actions. Leaders of exceptional intelligence and skill have always affected humanity in some way, shape, or form. They added pages to the history books and signed their names on our world with pens that are filled with courage.

Chosen vs. Self-Proclaimed Leadership

Throughout my travels around the world, I've had many deep discussions about various leaders from the past and present. These discussions last for hours on end and never seem to lose any energy or interest from all those conversing. In the discussions, there is always a brief moment when some of us are not in agreement with the leadership we've experienced within businesses, organizations, or politics. This burst of conflict in our discussion challenges us all to talk about our personal views from our specific leadership position. This is exactly what leadership development entails. It is an important role in your growth process. Connecting with leaders who will challenge your views helps you see another perspective from your leadership position. In turn, this will guarantee that your ego isn't bigger than the vision to help those who follow you. This willingness to engage with other viewpoints is a sure way to differentiate between chosen leaders and self-proclaimed leaders.

Chosen Leadership

The chosen ones are rarely understood by man . . .

Chosen, by definition, means having been selected as the best or most appropriate. All chosen leaders have something about them that can't be defined and measured, a certain *je ne sais quoi*. These leaders always exude an indescribable energy that their followers can easily feel through their words and actions. We've read about them in our history books and several certainly walk amongst us today. These leaders move with a sense of purpose and exhibit crystal-clear vision.

Self-Proclaimed Leadership

Personally speaking, I'm not a fan of this type of leadership because I've found that it actually isn't leadership at all. Being "self-proclaimed" is described as giving oneself a particular name or title, usually without any reason, merit, or endorsement by others. Regardless of how strong you are in certain areas that could make you a good leader, if you don't have someone to lead, you cannot be a leader. You must be supported by an individual or group to put your leadership attributes into action. How can anyone confirm that you're an effective leader if you've never had anyone to lead? Lack of confirmation, a track record, or a following equates to being a self-proclaimed leader.

I can recall watching a Harry Potter movie, *Chamber of Secrets*, when I recognized a self-proclaimed leader. Harry's teacher was considered a "famous author" amongst the wizards. He claimed to have accomplished many things and would tell stories of his past heroic moments. But there was no one to vouch for any of his so-called leadership abilities. And when an opportunity arose that called for a leader, he failed to rise to the challenge. Even worse, he failed miserably when he did step up. The school leaders and young students didn't respect him at all. They could see right through his "celebrity" image.

These "mis-leaders" can be found in our families, schools, society, movies and television programming, political systems, and in businesses throughout the world. It is our duty as leaders to show up, lead through actions, and let these self-proclaimed leaders do all the talking. Talking doesn't produce real and concrete results. Action is the engine that drives us to solve great problems and change the world.

Comparing Leadership Results

You can tell the difference between a chosen and a self-proclaimed leader through their actions and results. When chosen leaders are making moves, they ensure that their actions are for the greater good of their followers, their community. We can even say that they look into how their actions will affect humanity as a whole. We live in a global community. Even when focused on a local area, our actions can have a powerful effect on the global community as a whole. In contrast, self-proclaimed leaders try to find the spotlight more than find results. They are always looking for ways to build their brand, rather than building their business team, communities, and a better future for all humankind.

Throughout history, we see evidence of those who have received the mantle of leadership in the wrong manner, leaving a devastating effect on our businesses, organizations, communities, nations, and world. When a mis-leader with an overblown ego tries to prove his or her leadership instead of effectively leading, horrible things happen. Please don't misunderstand;

there are people, both young and old, who need the opportunity to show that they can lead. But when you have individuals with selfish visions and goals pursuing the opportunity to lead, it will eventually travel down a road of disaster. Chosen leaders don't need to yell from the mountaintop. They are aware of their abilities and proof of their skills can be seen in their actions. They make the necessary sacrifices to lead businesses, organizations, and humanity into prosperity.

Enhancing and Empowering Humanity

As leaders, we must continually remind ourselves that "it" is not about us. It has never been and it will never be. As leaders, our main goal, our sole focus, is to better our corresponding communities. You really must understand this statement, because if you forget, you will fall hard in the long run. When trust is lost in a leader, regaining that trust from your followers can be very, very difficult. To shatter the faith that your followers have in you means to shatter the entire foundation of what you all believe in. There is no room for mishaps.

Barry Schwartz, an American psychologist, stated the following during his speech "The Paradox of Choice": "If we are interested in maximizing the welfare of our citizens, the way to do that is to maximize individual freedom." Maximize individual freedom. Oh, how I agree! Freedom: the power or right to act, speak, or think as one wants without hindrance or restraint. As leaders, it is our responsibility to make sure the goals and visions that were birthed within us help to expand the freedom of other individuals.

Schwartz went on to say, "Freedom in itself is good, valuable, worthwhile, essential to being a human and if each person has freedom, we can each act on our own to maximize our entire welfare." When we speak about welfare, we are talking about the overall health, happiness, and fortune of a person and/or group. When we are truly effective in our leadership, not only do we enhance the welfare of others, but our very own welfare is affected as well. When you lead effectively, you're expanding freedom, establishing more and more "space" to allow all those who learn and receive guidance from us to grow. As they grow, they are able to assist in developing others and enrich the journey that we all take together.

"The way to maximize freedom is to maximize choice," Schwartz continues. A person of extraordinary leadership ability knows how to maximize and capitalize on the choices that are presented. When they capitalize effectively on said choices, they establish more freedom for themselves and others to develop and experience life. Thus begins the domino effect: more freedom begets healthier choices; healthier choices beget even more freedom, which creates a better welfare.

To achieve these goals and expand the land of freedom for the improved welfare of others, leaders must be clear and focused on a vision. Please note, the term "vision" is singular. One vision signifies a specifically set goal. There can and will be several avenues to achieve that goal, but still there can only be one common goal, one common vision. When you have your eyes set on the prize for multiple visions, you will falter. Your efforts and time spent will be wasted trying to accomplish multiple visions at once. Moreover, having multiple visions indicates that you, as a leader, have not simplified your foundation. What is your firm belief? What do you want your followers to believe in? They must have a clear and direct path in order for your vision to come to fruition. Without precise direction, you and your followers can and will be led astray.

Enhancement and empowerment complement each other. Having two agendas absolutely does not. Effective leadership means having one clear and defined vision. You must fully assess your vision to make sure you feel it in your gut. That is what you are taking lead to do—enhance and empower your global family: **humanity**.

Heavy Is the Head That Wears the Crown

Every title that you accept in your life carries the weight of responsibility. Some titles may hold more weight than others, but they all carry some responsibility just the same. When you take on a leadership position, you must be ready and willing to accept all that comes with it. "Heavy is the head that wears the crown" is a statement that has resonated with me from the moment I began to show true potential as a leader. To be fully honest, I didn't completely grasp the true meaning behind the statement until my ability to lead began being tested via rigorous challenges.

As a leader, everything you stand for will, at some point, be challenged, and may be even ridiculed. Not only will your ability to lead to higher levels be challenged, but your belief systems, your faith, your relationships, your lifestyle, and even your dreams and aspirations will be challenged. The list goes on and on. These challenges have the potential to break you down or build you up. The question you need to ask yourself is, AM I PREPARED? Many of you who are reading this book already know what I'm talking about. Day after day, you get up and you work and fight tirelessly to lead in your greatness—only to get up the next day, and the day after that, to do it all again. There is a spirit of tenacity that a true leader must possess to withstand these grueling challenges. It is not an easy task.

Recall when I discussed the difference between chosen leaders and self-proclaimed leaders. Well, this is where the real is separated from the fake. Everything that is claimed to be truth must be tested at some point. How else can it be proven as fact? When leaders begin to make progress, they move from the shallow waters into the deep oceans. It is there that they begin to deal with all types of sharks. These sharks can come in any form at any given time. Please note: "any given time" usually comes at a point when you feel most confident, most secure. Always be aware of your surroundings.

Leadership is a tough position. You will come across people who couldn't care less about how you personally feel or what you've been through while maintaining the weight of the crown's responsibility. Rest assured, you will have to deal with individuals who are selfish, egotistical, and have a hardened heart. There will be people who just don't want you to thrive. But you must remain steadfast, because remember, "it" is not about you. You took on this role to help, guide, and lead. Every great leader has a story of pain, agony, and defeat. I will share some of my own stories with you a little later on, but first I need you to understand that leadership is no walk in the park. You are not being crowned and asked to wave at your admirers. Far from it. You were chosen.

You accepted the opportunity you were given to conquer the goliaths whose sole purpose is to ruin your businesses, organizations, and communities, preventing them from reaching great heights. You were chosen to battle and defeat the sharks so that it would be safe for people to explore deeper parts of this great ocean of success. Heavy is the head that wears the crown, but those who are built to wear it do so with their heads high.

Here's to the Crazy Ones

"Here's to the crazy ones. The misfits. The rebels. The troublemakers. The round pegs in the square holes. The ones who see things differently. They're not fond of rules. And they have no respect for the status quo. You can quote them, disagree with them, glorify or vilify them. About the only thing you can't do is ignore them. Because they change things. They push the human race forward. And while some may see them as the crazy ones, we see genius. Because the people who are crazy enough to think they can change the world, are the ones who do."

—Rob Siltanen

CHAPTER 2

Transcending Leadership

*"A leader is one who knows the way,
goes the way, and shows the way."*

—John C. Maxwell

In my previous book, entitled, *Skyscraper: Going Beyond Your Limits to Reach Greatness,* I briefly discussed how it is essential for leaders of this generation and beyond to pursue transcendence in their actions. We live in a global community that seems much closer than it did ten or twenty years ago. We can thank technology for this, along with the leaders before us who broke barriers and went beyond the limits for the greater good.

To reiterate, to transcend means to be or go beyond the range or limits. The origin of the word is Latin: *transcendere,* which translates into across (trans) and climb (scandere). All transcending leaders, as evidenced through history, had to have a clear view of the mountains they were supposed to climb. Furthermore, they also needed to be able to climb, conquer, and go beyond those mountains. These leaders tapped into something within them that allowed them to change societies—to change cultures—beyond what we could have ever dreamed.

Transcending leaders and transformational leadership are synonymous. Leadership expert James MacGregor Burns introduced this concept back in 1978. He believed that leaders and followers allow each other to advance to a higher level of morality and motivation. "Transformational leadership" is defined as a style of leadership where the leader collaborates with followers (such as employees) to identify the needed change, creating a vision to guide the change through inspiration, and executing the change in tandem with committed members of the group. It also serves to enhance the motivation, morale, and job performance of followers through a variety of mechanisms; these include connecting the follower's sense of identity and self to the project and the collective identity of the organization; being a role model for followers in order to inspire them and enhance their interest in the project; challenging followers to take greater ownership of their work; and understanding the strengths and weaknesses of followers, allowing the leader to align individual followers with tasks that enhance their performance.

All of the great transcending leaders in our history were transformational in their leadership. They always pushed for collaborations with others because their mission was for the greater good. When people heard their speeches and watched them make decisions in moments of despair, it ignited a flame of passion regarding the situation at hand. Great leaders put actions behind their words. This is what changes the course of history for all who follow after.

Transcending with Authenticity

A prime character trait in a great leader is authenticity. The word "authentic" means genuine, real, or of an undisputed origin. It is vital that leaders prove authenticity when talking and interacting with those they lead. When in the public eye, it is of the utmost importance that you be yourself rather than put on a mask and act as if you received your position from a Hollywood casting agent. True leaders do not have to act or perform. They understand they are dealing with real-life situations, real-life emotions, and real-life decisions that will affect real people in real time.

Authentic leadership is a concept recently made popular by Harvard professor Bill George, who wrote, "Authentic Leadership is an approach to leadership that emphasizes building the leader's legitimacy through honest relationships with followers, which value their input and are built on an ethical foundation. Generally, authentic leaders are positive people with truthful self-concepts who promote openness. By building trust and generating enthusiastic support from their subordinates, authentic leaders are able to improve individual and team performance." When you are not forthright with your position, you will be scrutinized. The public is not very forgiving of inauthenticity.

Transcending with Humility

Humility is the quality or state of being humble—of knowing that, as humans, no man is above another and no man is better than another. Humility comes as you develop your skills over time. Some leaders learn through their losses, some in the development stages of becoming a leader, and some have the benefit of learning through their victories. A person who shows humility is able to preserve their legacy, power, and name beyond eternity. Humility is another powerful character attribute to have when walking the journey of leadership.

Being "in the spotlight" can be a very dangerous place for leaders if they don't know themselves. "The spotlight" creates an open playground for a person's ego to be set free to roam and destroy. Humility tames this brat, putting it in the corner for punishment. Too many times, we've watch leaders fall on the same sword that was supposed to protect us. It is always heartbreaking to see, but there we find the lesson of what happens when you don't lead with humility. As one of my own favorite mottos says: *"It's best to stay humble because you never know when you will fumble."*

Showing humility doesn't make you weak. It shows enlightenment. It shows that you recognize what is important and that you are aware that you are not the focus. Like I said a few pages back in the section, **Enhancing and Empowering Humanity**, "As leaders, we must continually remind ourselves that "it" is not about us. It has never been and it will never be." Leaders with humility are able to deal with the weight of the spotlight and to engage with the responsibilities that are most important. This is because they don't add the weight of their ego to the equation, which would result in disaster.

Transcending with Transparency

Transparency is a character trait all leaders should have. When a leader is transparent, they are forever consistent in their actions and behavior as a person of tremendous responsibility. They have a solid reputation for being honest, open, and trustworthy with those they have interacted with. Trust, a vital component to being a great leader, can only be achieved through consistency.

Leaders who demonstrate transparency allow others to share their opinions and have an in-depth dialog in complete honesty. In these modern times, leaders must understand that technology is a great ally to achieving transparency on a global scale.

Check out these quick tips to help you become more transparent:

- ☐ Recognize the times to be vulnerable. Expressing yourself openly allows others to do the same. If you want to receive trust, you must give honesty.

- ☐ Be consistent in your messages when speaking about your mission and goals. There should be no doubt coming from others about your stance on issues where you want others to follow you.

- ☐ Don't make promises. Simply keep your word. Nothing shows transparency more than an individual who can keep his or her word. Don't be the one making excuses about why you were late, or couldn't come out to support, or didn't follow through. Don't fall into this group. Work hard to be a person of your word.

- Listen to the opinions of others. Allow people to be just as honest as you would want them to allow you to be. Effective leaders listen. So stop talking and *listen*.

- Include others in the problem-solving strategy. Allow this to be part of your structure to communicate transparency. When you are effective in developing strategy and structure for transparent communication, you will have faster and more effective results.

"I always want a little dirt on my shoe. I always want one more stairwell to climb. I always want to walk up a walk-up. And not have an elevator built into my walk-up to survive. Because when you lose focus is when you forget. You forget how you got to the top, and once you forget how you got to the top, you forget everyone that helped you. And you forget everything that inspired you. And you wake up one morning and that inspiration and that creativity gives you one ol' middle finger that says, 'You forgot me. You denied me, and I'm the reason for you.'"

—LADY GAGA

CHAPTER 3

RahGor's 8 Principles for Leading with Humility

Here are my Eight Principles for Leading with Humility for all my fellow leaders. It's important to shape your thoughts to be humble. Take the time to review the eight principles and apply them however you see fit.

Principle #1: You Don't Know Everything

No matter how many victories you've won or how many people praise you, you must always remind yourself that you don't know everything. Be willing to delegate to the best people in the areas that you are weak in. Always be willing and open to learn from those who may not be from the same place as you, physically or mentally. Truth is not held in one location.

Principle #2: You're Not the Only One

If you believe that you are the only leader who can lead effectively, you will soon be very disappointed. You are not the only person making a change in the world. Be sure to give credit where credit is due. Be willing to learn from other leaders who are effectively making change on various levels. Learn to be a fan of others who are scoring also high points through leadership.

Principle #3: Don't Fall Victim to Praise

It is okay to appreciate and enjoy the praise you'll receive. But you must learn to pick up the trophy and put it back on the shelf so that your hands aren't occupied with holding it. Don't overindulge in the nice words people say about you and your work. Keep your focus on the work and mission. Too much time in the spotlight will burn you. Too much celebration will make you oversleep and miss your next opportunity to make a greater impact on the world.

Principle #4: Always Serve Others

Serving others is the bottom line, and will always be the core of any true leader's mission. You lead people to assist in the betterment of humanity and the planet on which we all live. The day you forget to serve others is they day they will forget about you. Remember, too: leaders can't influence people who don't pay any attention to them.

Principle #5: Listen More; Speak Less

It's important to know about the people you lead (or want to lead). You need to know and understand the areas in which they most need help. *Hear* them when they speak of what they desire—what they love and want to see more of in the world. It's never about you; it's always about them. If you can't take the time to know them, then who are you leading?

Principle #6: Question with Passion and Enthusiasm

Question everything like a child. Be excited to learn something new and to learn how things work. Show up to conferences, workshops, and meetings with enthusiasm to learn more, so you can do more. Let the energy of passion pour in and out of you as you learn from those who are expert in their work. You never know how the answers to your questions might elevate you to the next level.

Principle #7: The Community Chose You

Never forget that a collective group of people put you in the position to lead. You may have studied, made decisions, and realized a vision for the greater good of the people. But you didn't make yourself a leader; they allowed you to lead them. You can't lead without someone who accepts your vision as their own. You can't give speeches to an empty room and expect someone to hear you. No; the community you lead in allows you the honor and privilege of leading them.

Principle #8: Be a Student of Life

Always seek to be a student as long as you live. Never stop learning. Each generation will change the way we live. Technology will advance, as will the ways in which we learn. When you decide to be a permanent student in the school of life, you will always be better than you were yesterday. You can grow to be a better individual in society and you can grow to be a better person in leadership. Never stop learning and always implement what you learn so that you can also be a teacher to those who want to be a student.

CHAPTER 4

The (3) Commitments of a Leader

"Most men can stand adversity, very few men can stand success."

—Walter Sach

The Wealth of Effective Leadership

Over the years, I have quietly studied some of the greatest global organizational leaders from the entrepreneurial, political, corporate, and non-profit sectors. In my quest to be an effective entrepreneur and global leader, I knew that I had to be a devoted student and go through history to study the blueprints left behind by past leaders. My goal is to create a blueprint from my own journey that can be shared and studied amongst future potential entrepreneurs and global leaders. I want to add to the cycle of leadership.

The title of "leader" is a crown to be valued in the highest. During my studies, I recognized that passionate leaders received great praise and power in the areas they specifically focused on. While they may have had many ideas to implement in various areas, they remained focused. They didn't spread themselves thin and they knew how to delegate. They were visionaries who stayed strong in their principles. In today's society, there are far too many self-proclaimed leaders and individuals who invest more in their own egos than in the people who choose to follow them. This type of leadership stands on a flimsy foundation; it is weak, and can bear no weight. These mis-leaders propagate false hope and achieve very little to create a bright future for their organizations.

During my studies, I read that great leaders must commit to three things:

★ Value the people they lead

★ Relate to the people they value

★ Enhance the value of others

When a person leads by a **VALUE** to **RELATE** and **ENHANCE**, they become a leader. Thriving cultures are **PLAN** created by effective leadership. When leading an organization, you must be mindful that your organization's culture begins in the recruitment process. Great leaders lead in cultures that grow the talent needed. They don't look outside the group first; that should always be the last option.

When you are an effective leader, you will attract the following:

★ Passionate followers, members, or employees

★ Great individuals who can add to the value of your organization and culture

★ Loyalty and total devotion

You'll also be able to ensure that there's less bickering and internal politics in your group, because you'll be able to keep it out from the beginning by building a devoted following working together to achieve your vision.

You can receive a great deal of wealth when you are an effective leader—and it's not all of the monetary variety. Your human capital—your followers and the changes they can make in the world—is just as important to nurture as your financial capital. Your small company can become a Fortune 500 firm, your culture can begin to flourish, and you will be able to attract the best individuals, who will be more than willing to release their greatness on the platforms you lead. These are among of the results possible when you make a commitment to **VALUE, RELATE,** and **ENHANCE.**

Commitment #1: Value the people you lead

The word "value" **means** the regard that something is held to deserve; it is the importance, worth, or usefulness of that thing. Each person you lead must be valued as highly as a diamond around the neck of royalty. Leaders who do not value those who support them will eventually lose the value of their ability to lead. You must see yourself through the eyes of your supporters, as well as the eyes of your customers.

Far too often, individuals forget that a leadership position doesn't mean more spotlights for them. It means more spotlight to show the importance of those who give their valuable time, money, and attention to the missions you lead. When you see yourself through the eyes of those you lead, you treat them in the manner you would want to be treated. You take care of them just as you would take care of yourself. If you're new to your leadership position, you probably received it because you proved that you value your followers, team, and/or customers. A leadership position is a responsibility that should never be taken for granted. You are only a leader because your followers made you one.

Commitment #2: Relate to the value of others

The word "relate" means to show or make a connection; to understand and like or have sympathy for something. As a leader, you must strive to make a connection with the people you're serving. Making a connection allows you to understand how your decisions affect others. It also enhances the loyalty of your followers and customer base.

No leader can lead a group of people or industry without relating to the masses. The people want to know that they are supporting a person who understands their culture, their struggle, and their vision. Relating to the value of others shows your commitment to them, respect towards their belief system, and appreciation to their way of life. Mutual respect and circle of intimate trust is shared among the people because the value you see in them is reflected in your passion to enhance their lives.

Commitment #3: Enhance the value of others

The word "enhance" means to intensify, increase, or further improve the quality, value, or extent of something. Effective leaders commit without hesitation to the enhancement of those around them. To lead is to develop, and to develop is to become more. If you are able to enhance the lives of others around you, you are an extraordinary leader. But it doesn't stop there; great leaders have a need to continually develop themselves to be able to enhance the lives of others.

As great leaders, when we spend time enhancing value in others, we must know exactly what needs to be enhanced and developed so that we can give precise information, tools, products, and guidance. This leads to an effective development effort. Development is a wonderful journey for leaders. It is a time for us to be inspired by change and to change ourselves. We lead to help others live better lives. We are all given this one life and we should always value this gift so that we can strive to live and lead better than we did yesterday.

> *"The sage does not hoard. The more he helps others, the more he benefits himself. The more he gives to others, the more he gets himself. The Way of Heaven does one good but never does one harm. The Way of the sage is to act but not to compete."*
>
> —Lao Tzu

IF

By Rudyard Kipling

If you can keep your head when all about you
    Are losing theirs and blaming it on you,
If you can trust yourself when all men doubt you,
    But make allowance for their doubting too;
If you can wait and not be tired by waiting,
    Or being lied about, don't deal in lies,
Or being hated, don't give way to hating,
    And yet don't look too good, nor talk too wise:

If you can dream—and not make dreams your master;
    If you can think—and not make thoughts your aim;
If you can meet with Triumph and Disaster
    And treat those two impostors just the same;
If you can bear to hear the truth you've spoken
    Twisted by knaves to make a trap for fools,
Or watch the things you gave your life to, broken,
    And stoop and build 'em up with worn-out tools:

If you can make one heap of all your winnings
    And risk it on one turn of pitch-and-toss,

And lose, and start again at your beginnings
    And never breathe a word about your loss;
If you can force your heart and nerve and sinew
    To serve your turn long after they are gone,
And so hold on when there is nothing in you
    Except the Will which says to them: "Hold on!"

If you can talk with crowds and keep your virtue,
    Or walk with Kings—nor lose the common touch,
If neither foes nor loving friends can hurt you,
    If all men count with you, but none too much;
If you can fill the unforgiving minute
    With sixty seconds' worth of distance run,
Yours is the Earth and everything that's in it,
    And—which is more—you'll be a Man, my son.

CHAPTER 5

The Servant Entrepreneur

"The strongest brand has a giving hand."
—RAHGOR

I recall an inspiring call with a friend who had just returned home from a two-week meditation retreat. We are both entrepreneurs, so of course there were moments in the conversation where we discussed the importance of enhancing ourselves so that we could then enhance those we serve through our businesses. After my friend shared with me his daily routine during the retreat, the word "servant" replayed over and over in my head. I remember telling him why it's important that we, as leaders, should invest in ourselves daily in order to be assets in the lives of those we serve. We must be transcendent **"servant entrepreneurs"** if we want to change the world.

A **servant**, by definition, means a person who performs duties for others. That person is a devoted and helpful follower or supporter. An **entrepreneur** is a person who organizes and operates a business or businesses, taking on greater than normal risks personally, financially, and so on. Thus, a **servant entrepreneur** strives to plan, establish, and operate a strong business structure that provides transcendent service and/or products; their success rate is validated by the amount of lives that have been permanently changed through their work.

Entrepreneurs take an extraordinary risk to provide a service or product, a risk that is only possible when the individual has unwavering faith and courage in service or product. But even with these two attributes, many entrepreneurs still fail due to a lack of strategic planning, lack of research and development, lack of an understanding of their target market and the culture of their customers, or lack of quality services. As a servant entrepreneur, you give your all so that you can reach beyond the norm. You strive to fill the areas where people are lacking because you want the best for your customers and clients. You know that if you slack in an area that should be your strongest, you are doing a disservice to the people who trust that you will supply a quality product or service.

This is another form of leadership in action; servant entrepreneurs definitely lead and strive for growth through service. No matter what business or organization we create, it's never about us. It is about the individuals we serve, and how we directly affect them for long-term change.

Caroline Myss, author of *Anatomy of Spirit*, said, "Most people lead their lives following a course that is not their own. And unless you can find the course that is truly your own, you will remain off course." I've created seven pillars that I believe will help keep you on course as a servant entrepreneur. As you embrace these seven pillars, ask yourself, "What or how can I serve in the most innovative and inspiring way to as many people in the world as possible?"

7 Pillars of a Servant Entrepreneur

Servant Entrepreneur Pillar #1

Measure the quality of your service or product by how many lives it enhances. *(The strongest brand has quality in the giving hand.)*

Servant Entrepreneur Pillar #2

Be precise: have a clear understanding of your mission and sense of purpose. *(This attracts more helping hands to expand your land.)*

Servant Entrepreneur Pillar #3

Nurture fruitful growth. *(This allows you to be a constant resource and asset in your business and personal life.)*

Servant Entrepreneur Pillar #4

Embrace the honor and responsibility to lead the next generation of entrepreneurs. *(This is confirmation of your wealth of influence.)*

Servant Entrepreneur Pillar #5

Always be authentic and honest. *(This validates your integrity.)*

Servant Entrepreneur Pillar #6

Treat humanity as family. *(This enhances your level of communication and compassion for all those around you.)*

Servant Entrepreneur Pillar #7

Focus on the well-being of the people you serve daily. *(This pushes you to provide the best service and products possible.)*

CHAPTER 6

Establishing and Nurturing a Culture of Success

Here, I would like to briefly touch on the topic of culture. As a leader, you must remember that you are investing in the culture you lead (even if you weren't aware of it until now). Culture is known as the arts and other manifestations of human intellectual achievement regarded collectively; it also refers to how a group interacts with each other and with the world. Culture is how people in a collective group develop and/or assist in finding a way of communicating a living part of their lifestyle.

Vision and Message of Your Culture

I had a discussion with my uncle some time ago about the direction I was moving with my company and my awesome team. We talked about the importance of having a precise vision and he told me, "The greatest leaders can articulate a vision. Martin Luther King Jr. was able to articulate a vision of freedom and equality. He could excite people to create a reality of the vision they each held in their mind."

Ask yourself, "What type of culture am I creating? What type of people am I attracting and developing in this leadership position?" This opens your eyes to what type of message you are putting out into the world and how you may be perceived by those you are trying to attract to your organization—and to your vision.

Establishing a vision and articulating it to the individuals you want to attract is how building a culture begins. Culture then spawns into various detailed branches of the group. If you don't have a solid vision, you will have a weak foundation and the message about who you are, the people you lead, and the vision you think you have will be open to misinterpretation. Remember this:

> *"Thoughts are like water, they flow*
> *everywhere at all times. But when you freeze*

a thought and focus on it completely, it becomes solid, like water turning to ice."

The culture you create thrives or dies based on the strength of the vision you articulate. When you have a clear and solid vision, it creates a clear path for others to come together to help create and accomplish shared goals. Remember this as an equation:

Clear Vision + Realistic Goals = Culture in Motion

The people you lead will not value any goals you establish unless they are in agreement with your vision. Again, people support you when they are in support of your vision—when they RELATE.

Your Team, Your Culture

Your team is a great reflection of your leadership and how ideas, plans, and directions are created and executed. Your organization's culture is defined by how this group of people is managed and handled. For example, the manner in which the phone is answered is a reflection of your organizational culture. So is the attire and paraphernalia that your team wears and the attitude of your team when interacting with your followers.

Every part of your organization is both reflected in and reflective of your culture.

The very first experience a new team member has with your culture is usually during the interview process. This is the first impression for someone who is requesting to be part of the team; here, they can get a feel for what they are about to embark upon. Is your team more laid-back or fast-paced when it comes to completing work? During development, is your team more open or closed to opinions and innovation from its members? Does the leader (that's you) take time to get to know and assist in developing everyone's talents and skills? When searching for additions to your team, just looking for "help" will attract the wrong people. Be sure to seek out a person who will complement your team and your vision.

Pay Attention to the Details of Work Ethic

Be mindful of how you work and how your team perceives it. Then keep in mind how the outside world views the inner circle of your leadership team. It means and says a lot. You have a great vision, but if your work ethic is perceived as weak, the culture will lack influence and you will have no productive hands to help you build a prosperous future. Does everyone (including you) show up to meetings on time or late? Do you start those meetings on time? Do your clients or the people you serve feel awesome, intimidated, or careless around you? Why is this so? The actions of everyone who is part of the vision (including your followers) clearly reflect the culture of your business and organization. If everyone's movement and actions are strong, your culture will undoubtedly nurture success. If these actions are weak, you have two options: 1) Reset your organization to start from scratch and create the necessary strong foundation with your own work ethic; or 2) Start looking for a new position, because effective leadership is not your niche.

A Past Culture of Success

> *"Engaging the hearts, minds, and hands of talent is the most sustainable source of competitive advantage."*
>
> —Greg Harris, Quantum Workplace

I've been digging deep to learn how dynamic businessmen from the 1800s through the 1990s built their businesses from scratch. These businessmen each cultivated a special culture that allowed their organization to thrive during the highs and lows of business history.

During my research, I became a huge fan of the **early years** of Goldman Sachs business culture. The rawness, discipline, ambition, and visionary leaders the culture attracted was second to none.

The individual in the early Goldman Sachs culture who most intrigued me was Sidney Weinberg. In 1907, Weinberg started as a janitor's assistant with Goldman Sachs for the salary of a mere $3 per week; his responsibilities included brushing the firm partners' hats and wiping the mud from their shoes. Soon, Weinberg managed to impress Paul J. Sachs, the grandson of the firm's founder, who promoted him to the mailroom. Taking the initiative in his new role, Weinberg reorganized the mailroom, impressing Sachs yet again. Sachs offed the young man another opportunity: he sent him to Brooklyn's Browne's Business College to improve his penmanship. From there, the sky was the limit. Weinberg worked his way up to senior partner and became known as Mr. Wall Street.

It's important not to overlook the success-driven culture that was developed within the Sachs organization to reward hard work, dedication, and leadership, which allowed someone like Sidney Weinberg to start out as janitor's assistant, only to become one of the most dynamic senior partner of a well-respected global firm at that time. The values cultivated by a culture have an immense impact on an organization and on both its leaders and its team. I have compared many business cultures, such as that of Sachs, in various industries. It inspired me to create a list of characteristics for success that I believe will help entrepreneurs, CEOs, and organizational leaders in their pursuit of building a great culture of success in business. The culture of success can be created by anyone who truly takes time to nurture it from within!

RahGor List for a Culture of Success

Begin with the interview process

Every person who interviews for an open position in your company will make their own determination on how things work in your company. If the interview seems weak, so shall the mindset and view of your company in the interviewee's eyes.

Remember, the interview process is a business culture's first impression.

Inspire loyalty and total devotion

It is important that each person becomes inspired by the culture to show great loyalty and

> devotion. This is very important to the business during moments of success, as well as times of failure. This shows the culture's strength and the faith each person has in the value of the business.

Keep the politics out

Politics is defined as the activities associated with the governance of a country or other area, especially the debate or conflict among individuals or parties having or hoping to achieve power.

When creating a culture of success, there should be less of a focus on gaining power and more on empowering. Give someone the authority or power to do something. Focus on making someone stronger and more confident, especially when it comes to controlling their own life and claiming their rights. Give people a chance to become effective leaders.

Don't tolerate greed and ego

> The most important aspect of a business is the clients. It is important that the entire organization understands this central focus. This includes the leader of the pack as well.

Ego will lead you to fall on your own sword and greed will make sure you can't pull it out.

Build a sense of family

Creating a sense of family within an organization allows communication to flow gracefully. It will give each person a sense that they are a part of something bigger, more important than merely a place that gives them a paycheck. Everyone should feel like they are needed and like they play an important role in how the company (family) will grow and succeed.

Grow your talent from within

Prosperity in business takes time. Having someone who knows the entire organization from the inside and out is a true asset. You must remember that no one washes the rental car. This means that if you hire someone who doesn't truly know the culture or history of your business, they may not take pride in your business like someone who started as a janitor and rose to become a senior partner in a global firm.

Never go on sale

Let's get this straight from the start. **Your life is valuable.** This means **your thoughts are valuable.** This means **your visions are valuable.** This means **everything you say and create in this world has value.** This is why you should never settle for less in anything you do. When you are sure of who you are and the destination you are trying to reach, why would you bargain for less? Honestly, why would you waste your time bargaining in the first place when you are fully aware of your worth?

Take a lesson from high-end fashion designers such as Louis Vuitton, Gucci, and Valentino. Before, during, and after the recession (and even to this day), they have never lowered their prices on any of their clothing, shoes, or accessories. You don't see commercials on TV promoting "one-day sales" or holiday specials for these brands, or even see a sale rack in their stores. Why? It's because they know the value of their company, the value of their vision, and the value of their target clients. These designers know that their fashion designs, visions, and connections are too valuable to be watered down for people who would only buy their products at a cheaper cost, rather than paying what they're worth.

Use this as an example for your own life. Never lower your standards or put your vision up for sale. Don't accept or agree to things that belittle your value.

You deserve the best out of life and you need to make sure you are treated with high regard. If other people allow others to treat their life as an 80% off sale rack, then that's their decision. You have to understand that there are many people who are content with buying and flaunting the fake for half-off rather than buying and dealing with the real for full price, no matter what the benefits.

Not everyone deserves your valuable time and attention (especially if you are making major moves on your journey). People will treat you cheaply if you let them. If they don't treat their own lives with respect, what makes you think they would treat yours with any? My life, my vision, my time, and my attention aren't cheap. And because of this, I will never give out coupons and never go on sale.

Don't aim to be less

To be aimless means to have no goal, purpose, or direction. You've heard people complain about how there isn't enough time in the day to do the things they "chose" to put on their To-Do List. But rarely will you hear someone tell you excitedly about the strategies they formulated to tackle their one big goal or why all the listed activities on their To-Do List will help them become a master of their craft.

It all comes down to having clear vision and understanding which activities should be held as priorities. Todd Henry, author of *Die Empty*, said, "Priorities are difficult. When you choose one thing to focus on, you automatically choose not to focus on others. This is why some people fall into aimlessness: they don't like the discomfort of having to say no to very good things that aren't the *most* important things. They'd rather be mediocre at a lot of things than take a real swing at things they care about and risk failure."

Below are some tips to help you get out of the aimlessness hole—or not fall into it in the first place. It is vital that you understand that whatever value you put on various daily activities shines a truthful light on your standards for living a productive, honest, and radiant life.

Tip #1 – Start at the End

See the vision you want to make a reality and ask yourself, "What productive actions *must* I take to bring this into fruition?" Be honest with yourself.

Tip #2 - Busy Does Not Mean Productive

After you make your To-Do List for the day, ask yourself what will happen once you finish each task.

If it will not bring you closer to achieving the overall vision, take it off the list. PERIOD!

Tip #3 - Finish What You Started

There may be projects and issues that you must complete/solve, even if you don't want to—HANDLE IT! This may be what's holding you back from appreciating and feeling great about making your vision a reality.

Tip #4 - Be a General and Fight Your Battles

Nothing comes easy for the things we yearn for. When things get tough, fight through the emotions. Don't let your emotions, others' opinions, or the "greener grass on the other side" mentality deter you from completing the task at hand.

Tip #5 - Describe Your Vision in Detail

Envision what you will be wearing, who will be around you, what seasons you will experience, how high your energy will be, what you will get rid of, what you will attract. Know your vision and make sure you are just as excited as the kid who walks into the candy store. It's your vision. It's a priority. And it should be the focused target that steers you away from aimlessness.

THE WISE OLD MAN

A wealthy man requested an old scholar wean his son away from his bad habits. The scholar took the youth for a stroll through a garden. Stopping suddenly, he asked the boy to pull out a tiny plant growing nearby.

The youth held the plant between his thumb and forefinger and pulled it out easily. The old man then asked him to pull out a slightly bigger plant. The youth pulled hard and the plant came out, roots and all. "Now pull out that one," said the old man, pointing to a bush. The boy had to use all his strength to pull it out.

"Now take this one out," said the old man, indicating a sturdy guava tree. The youth grasped the trunk and tried to pull it out, but it would not budge. "It's impossible," complained the boy, panting with the effort.

"So it is with bad habits," said the sage. "When they are young, it is easy to pull them out, but when they take hold, they cannot be uprooted."

That session with the old man changed the boy's life.

Moral: Don't wait for bad habits to grow in you. Pull them out by the roots while you have control over them. Otherwise, they will control you.

CHAPTER 7

The Great Power of Ten

I am a true student of the late, great Jim Rohn. He has taught millions of people all over the world about leadership and personal development. There is no way that I could write this book without highlighting some of the insights I received from the master of personal development through his books and videos. As leaders, we must continuously work to be masters of our thoughts and actions. It is through our mastery of self that we can unleash our true power and be dynamic in all that we do.

In one of Jim Rohn's lectures, he talked about the ten great powers. The ten great powers are focused on self-development. Remember, in order to develop others, you first have to develop yourself. I would like to share my notes on these ten powers for the benefit of helping you become a more impactful global leader.

1. The Power in Purpose

Each of us was created to fulfill some type of purpose on this earth. Each day, we are on a different mission to fulfill that purpose in life. When we understand ourselves, we always have a sense of what that greater purpose is, but each day we focus on the activities that have to be done to get there. There will be successes and failures over the course of these missions. But there is nothing to stress about even in those failed missions, because there is always a lesson to be learned. This is part of fulfilling our purpose as well.

As effective global leaders, we must lead with a sense of purpose. We must lead with a sense of fulfillment that will pull us to a place of strength, which is where we need to take others. When things become massively tiring and difficult, we can look within to gain the strength necessary to push forward. Leading with purpose allows great global leaders to reside in a different realm. They take all those who follow them beyond the limits they set for themselves. They are living examples of empowerment, leading with an unwavering faith to fulfill their purpose.

2. The Power in Self Confidence

Self-confidence means a feeling of trust in one's abilities, qualities, and judgment. Your inner strength will always be there to rely on when things get tough. It is completely your responsibility to do the best you can every day in order to keep a positive attitude and outlook during your journey in life. The joy and love you yearn for start with you, inside you. Cultivate the joy, love, strength you need to get through the days (tough or not). These three attributes are all you need to accomplish your goals.

Confidence is your ability to make decisions, provide support for others, and trust in your God-given talents. There are droves of people who want to do more, accomplish more, maybe even lead, but who lack the belief that they can do it. When people try to bring you down and no one wants to support what you are trying to do, that's when your self-confidence should be at its highest level. You know your purpose. Find your strength from within and release that self-confidence.

3. The Power in Enthusiasm

Consider enthusiasm another necessity as you continue to develop and take this journey as a leader. Jim Rohn stated that enthusiasm is 90% on the inside and 10%

on the outside. (I wasn't lying when I said all that you need starts from within you.) Although enthusiasm is intense and eager enjoyment, its alternate side is subtle and quiet dedication. Enthusiasm is attached to your driven purpose and cultivated by your self-confidence.

When you see the true effect of helping others, your enthusiasm is triggered. Your enthusiasm is pure energy, so it will branch off and affect all who bear witness to it. You will need enthusiasm in all that you do as a leader. This helps to attract others, encouraging them to want to know more about you and your mission. Enthusiasm will help you get through the tough moments and give the pull that keeps you focused and excited about the work you are doing. You can (and should) tap into this source of energy whenever you need to, because there will always be much work that needs to be done. And what better way to attack it than with enthusiasm!

4. The Power in Expertise

Yearning to be the best is not a bad thing. I do believe it's important to excel in your skill set and with the talents you possess. However, trying to be the best simply to impress others is unhealthy. Oftentimes, people aren't satisfied with or impressed by what others do for them, even when it's done in the best way possible. To excel in various skills and not settle for regular, ordinary, or average is where your power lies.

As a leader, especially a global leader, it's important to strive toward excellence in all ways possible. Your focus should always be on developing your skills and characteristics to become the most exceptional leader, man/woman, and human being possible. Push to be an expert in achieving excellence. You should be the best expert on yourself. Instead of pushing to be better than others, push to be a better you than you were yesterday. You can become a supreme being if you continue to develop yourself with unrelenting passion.

5. The Power in Preparation

Preparation is a process that should be treated with the highest regard. The reason I say this is because we make future decisions based upon the plans and strategies we created yesterday and today. The decisions you make *during* your preparation will determine your success. In your preparation process, you should question every area of yourself and the route you want to take to achieve your missions and goals.

We do not receive what we want; we only receive what is beneficial to our current path. That is how this universe is aligned for our lives. There is a reaction for every action. Weak actions produce weak reactions (results). A lack of preparation will eventually result in you faltering. And be certain: if, by chance, you do happen to receive something of value as a result of your weak planning, it will not be long-lived.

Every value in life must be compensated for in some way. This is the law of the universe: Give and you shall receive. For what you seek, you shall find. Always prepare yourself for whatever may come. Be ready for the challenges and opportunities that may arise. Then, even if all that you assumed never happens, at least you were prepared for it. Be of ACTION.

6. The Power in Self-Reliance

Leaders must be self-reliant, relying on their own powers and resources rather than those of others. You must primarily rely on yourself to be more and do more. You have a personal responsibility and commitment to trust that you have the ability to get things done. You are the headstone. Know when and who to delegate to. But understand that your support system can only do so much for you.

Having self-reliance means that you don't whine or complain about the actions you take. You know things have to get done and that the goals you set for yourself are for you alone to achieve. Even when your goal is to help others, you still have to be able to assume the various positions needed to reach that goal. Take responsibility for the necessary actions. If others can't do something and you know it's important, make the decision to bring the task to completion. Rely on your strength and inner power. Never complain and never explain.

7. The Power in Image

How people see you as you fulfill the leadership position is important. Showing an image of control and goal orientation is powerful. You will be more attractive and influential when you project an image of productivity and importance. Your image is formulated by how you talk, dress, and develop over time. Studies show that 93% of communication is nonverbal, and so having a strong visual representation of your message, purpose, and mission is critical.

People always look for someone or something to believe in. Young people are more visual than anything else. Think about those two things together. How does your image inspire and attract people to follow you to accomplish goals? "Imagery" means visually descriptive or in a figurative language, especially in literary work; presenting the right imagery can make a huge difference in how you are perceived and, therefore, in how effective you can be as a leader. But what's most important is how you appear to yourself, because if you fail to impress yourself, it will be very difficult to impress others.

8. The Power of Character

Character is an area of importance as a leader no matter what level you are on the leadership pole. You must continuously develop the inner you. You must be a person of principle and honesty. You must be a person of integrity; this adds value to your character. Developing your character (for the better, of course) will earn you the respect of others. People don't just give you their attention and valuable time unless they feel you're worthy of it.

A person's character—their reputation—always precedes them. This includes leaders and people of great stature in society. Your character will always be evaluated and scrutinized. Establishing a set of principles or pillars in your life helps you to unleash your inner power. Almost certainly, others around you will want to assist and provide the space that you need to showcase your ability to lead. Invest in yourself and develop the supreme character in you!

9. The Power of Self-Discipline

Self-discipline is one of my strongest areas, so I'm excited to delve into this subject with you! Having self-discipline means having the ability to control one's feelings and overcome one's weaknesses; it's the ability to pursue what one thinks is right despite temptations to abandon it. Having self-discipline will take you farther than many of the people you come across in your life. People are influenced and easily distracted by things that hinder them from advancing in life. You must have a strong work ethic and be self-disciplined to bring the task(s) to completion and uphold your responsibilities.

You must be strong in your development because people are counting on you. Being self-disciplined also means being self-motivating. You shouldn't have to rely on anyone or anything to direct you on what you know needs to be done. Knowing how important your role is to the entire vision is what great leaders understand and focus on. Your power lies in self-discipline. This means that every day, you are relentless in your work ethic and the execution of your plans. You are aware and in control of your emotions so that you can complete the given tasks set in front of you. You are able to stay away from temptations and suppress your ego. Self-discipline is what separates the best from the rest.

10. The Power in Developing Extraordinary Performance

To live and lead extraordinarily, you must first recognize what you want and what you are capable of doing. Any great accolade was due to great work ethic. You must do what most will not so that you can see and experience what most will not. Each of the 10 powers that I've outlined (including this one) can bring about some of the most profound experiences and results, taking you beyond the limits of the average. There is no such thing as being average, thinking average, working average, and still having extraordinary results. No way!

You have to take extraordinary measures to lead with greatness. You can walk and lead with influence when you embody the characteristics that captivate all those around you. Extraordinary, by definition, means very unusual or remarkable. How remarkable is your work ethic? How unusual is your energy to achieve the unachievable? Demand of yourself to be extraordinary. No one but you can make you extraordinary or do the things that make your experience extraordinary. Demand it. Be it. Be illuminated by it. Make extraordinary your ordinary.

The Gardener's Badge Story

A landscape gardener ran a business that had been in the family for two or three generations. The dedicated staff would work on gardens or make deliveries—anything from bedding plants to ride-on mowers. The staff was happy and customers loved to visit the store.

For as long as anyone could remember, the current owner and previous generations of owners had been extremely positive, happy people.

Most folk assumed it was because they ran a successful business.

In fact, it was the other way around . . .

The owner was notorious for always wearing a big lapel badge that exclaimed, **"Business Is Great!"**

The business was indeed generally great, although it went through tough times like any other. But one thing that never changed was the owner's attitude and that enormous badge, **Business Is Great!**

Everyone who saw the badge for the first time invariably asked, "What's so great about business?" Sometimes people would confide that their own business was miserable, or even that they personally were miserable or stressed out.

Regardless, the **Business Is Great!** badge tended to always start a conversation, which typically involved the owner talking about several positive aspects of business and work, for example:

- ★ The pleasure of meeting and talking with different people every day

- ★ The reward that comes from helping staff take on new challenges and experiences

- ★ The fun and laughter in a relaxed and healthy work environment

- ★ The fascination of the work itself

- ★ The joyful feeling when you finish a job, having done it to the best of your ability

- ★ The new things you learn every day—even without looking to do so

- ★ And the thought that everyone in business is blessed—because there are many millions of people who would swap their own situation to have the same opportunities of having a productive, meaningful job, in a civilized, well-fed country, where, honestly, there are no real worries.

And so the list went on. And no matter how miserable a person was, they usually ended up feeling a lot happier after just a few minutes of listening to all this infectious enthusiasm and positivity.

It is impossible to quantify or measure attitude like this, but to one extent or another, it would seem to be a self-fulfilling prophecy. Occasionally, when asked about the badge in a quiet moment, the business owner would confide:

"The badge came first. The great business followed."

CHAPTER 8

Measuring Your Impact

Your impact in the areas that you focus on must be measured so that you can see where you are most effective. If you don't take the necessary steps to measure your impact, you will never know if you are leading in the right direction. You will never know if people are truly experiencing change with you as the person making the decisions. When we are cooking and baking, we use measuring cups to make sure we add the right amount of ingredients to make everything taste good. Even those who are professional cooks and bakers have ways of measuring ingredients, even if they don't use measuring utensils all the time.

Measurement is important because you need to make sure you are examining the right information, investing the best energy, giving the best direction, and actually seeing the well-being of others increase in the most positive way. When you don't measure the impact of your actions and investments in others, it's like giving directions with a blindfold on, hoping that you pointed everyone in the right direction. This is not what you want to be doing as a leader. A leader understands that the right measurements of ingredients results in a well-fed community.

How to Measure Your Impact

Having a proper structure in place for impact measurement is a brilliant way of making sure you are leading effectively. Below are a few ways that you can measure your impact periodically to make sure that you are making positive strides. Feel free to add to this list by coming up with creative activities and strategies of your own.

Measurement #1: Perception of Leadership

You can measure your impact by the amount of attention your leadership receives from those who follow you. They give attention by giving you awards, media exposure, praise for your dedication and work, and opportunities to speak about whatever your leadership position represents. These days, even your social media can play a big role in the perception and impact of your leadership. Your leadership presence and perception can be measured by these things because perception deals with the ability to see, hear, or become aware of something through the senses.

Measurement #2: Team Performance

Every leader has a team that they can invest in and rely on to accomplish common goals. Measuring your team's performance from where they were "then" to where they are now is a great estimate of your impact. Measure their level of responsibilities and the development in their skill and talents. Measure if their communication is more effective amongst each other and with those they are helping you to lead. As a leader, you must be held accountable for affecting your team by assisting in enhancing the talents and skills they are bringing to the table.

Measurement #3: Growth in Following

When you are an effective leader, your impact will be reflected strongly in the amount of people who allow you to take the lead. If you gain one or 100 new supporters of your mission, purpose, or goal, rest assured you've made an impact.

Measurement #4: Set Milestones

Set short-term goals so that you can use them as milestones along the way. Celebrating your achievements on your journey is vital to the morale of your entire team (including you). Set these short-term goals realistically, but make sure they are set with enthusiasm. There is nothing worse than a goal that is so boring that its only impact will be everyone jumping ship—even the captain (that would be you).

Measurement #5: Enhancement in Attitude and Behavior

You can measure your impact by observing the attitudes and belief systems of those you are helping. Are they geared to be positive or negative? Consider what is being said and the reactions to statements you've made, directions you've taken, etc. Since you've been in your leadership position, has their belief system changed for the better or worse?

Measurement #6: Formation of Relationships

Relationships are a vital component to leadership. It should be a goal of all leaders to nurture and invest in relationships. To measure the impact of your leadership, review your database and see who is in your contact list. When you first started in your leadership role, you may have only had the corner store clerk in there. But now, as the years have come and gone, surely you've collected numerous contacts. (Check out the theory of Six Degrees of Separation.) You may have individuals who lead global organizations and help lead countries. You can measure your level of impact by whom you have dialog with and who you can reach out to when you are aiming to solve some of the problems on your list.

Measurement #7: Enhancement in Opportunities

There may have been a time when you had very few opportunities. But now, you must come to terms with the fact that you may have to turn some down. This is a great way to measure the impact of your leadership. When you are effective in your execution as a leader, there will be numerous requests for your words, your support, and your presence. This is a positive impact of leadership.

Measurement #8: Spark in Innovation

When you begin to see more and more ideas being innovated by your team and being supported (maybe even imitated) by those outside of your leadership circle, you can measure that as a positive. Innovation stems from the excitement and motivation of achieving something grand. Innovation is born in the environments where ideas are praised and given the golden ticket to run free. Leaders who can create the space and inspire the morale necessary for innovation have made the kind of impact that all leaders yearn to create. Innovation takes things to another level and pushes the human spirit to go beyond what is known.

Measurement #9: Enhancement in Organizational Structure and Function

When your impact is moving in the right direction, you will begin to see the growth in your team as well as in those that follow you. You must always be aware of when structure and function needs to be evolved.

You may have to add people to your team, supply and demand may increase, and you may be called to do more in the world.

Measurement #10: Increased Collaboration

Most recognizable when it comes to measuring impact are your collaborations. When aiming to make a greater impact, you can always collaborate with others who are interested in the same goal. The measurement comes when you notice that you are a contributing member of several collaborations or are receiving invitations to be a contributor. However you are involved with such collaborations, you can bet the house it is a positive measurement of impact.

Measurement #11: Duplication of Leadership Style and Brand

Measuring your impact can also involve examining the manner in which people duplicate your style of leadership. This measurement can be taken in one of two ways. Either you will 1) be offended that the other person is hijacking your style, or 2) you will be flattered by the fact that someone thought so highly of you that they tried their best to be just like you. I am always flattered when I see individuals trying to do something I've done or move the way I move. Think about the fashion designers who have created some of the most beautiful pieces. There are companies and individuals that seek to do the exact same thing because of the impact of those originals. Most times, though, people will refer back to the originator of that style. Now that's measurement with positive taste.

Leveraging Your Impact

Leveraging your leadership impact will assist in ensuring the longevity of your influence so that you can be a greater asset to those in need of guidance. When you have actual proof that your leadership capabilities are impactful, find ways to share your gift. This will create an ever-growing circle of connections for you, some of which whom will open even more doors for you to make more connections to nurture more relationships. You want to leverage your impact for three main reasons:

★ Influence current and potential leaders to work with you in some capacity

- ★ Bring attention to those in need so that you can help them in areas where you are most effective

- ★ Attract more talented people to your leadership team

By leveraging your impact, you have the upper hand in creating platforms for others. You will add more value to your brand, unleash your skills and talents, gain endorsements from highly respected fellow leaders, and earn great respect from those who follow you.

How RahGor Measures Impact

I want to briefly share about how we measure our impact with the RahGor brand. When we go into a new community or country, we evaluate all the issues that many of the locals talk about. We look at the business, political, and educational sectors. It is important that we acknowledge what the people whom we will be serving are dealing with. We want to know what is working well, what is not working, and what needs work.

For example, when we moved into one of our office buildings, I walked up and down the street to see how many homeless people occupied it. It was a personal goal (which almost immediately became a team goal) to figure out how we could make sure that there was not one homeless person on the street in which we housed our business, as part of our larger goal of improving the lives of those around us. One of the projects we created is called "Portraits of Serving." We provide food, clothing, and a copy of one of my published books for the homeless. We have individual conversations with people on the street to hear their stories about how homelessness became their reality. It is so very important to first know WHY a problem exists. This creates a clear path for us to come together to figure out HOW we can solve the problem.

I share this with you because my team and I recognized that if we have the actual facts and stats of what life is like before and after RahGor enters a particular community, this could be one of our measures of influence in that area. I am an entrepreneur, but I am also a global leader and it is a must that I leave my mark wherever I do business. So before you act, gather all the data, set up an effective strategy, set milestones (short-term goals), and be relentless in your actions.

The Bell Teacher

A new student approached the Zen master and asked how he should prepare himself for his training.

"Think of me as a bell," the master explained. "Give me a soft tap, and you will get a tiny ping. Strike hard, and you'll receive a loud, resounding peal."

CHAPTER 9

Who Will Save the Super Heroes?

I believe I am a superhero. Yes, I believe there are real-life superheroes in our world. In my previous book, *Skyscraper*, I discuss the difference between the role model and the superhero. I believe that superheroes are the real leaders of the world. They actually do the things other people sit and dream about. They are radical in faith and action (I'll get into that in the next chapter). Superheroes lead with such an extraordinary passion and determination that people have to wonder, "How did they manage to accomplish this huge goal?" or "When do they have the time to make things happen?" These leaders, these superheroes, present with such strong willpower that people forget the battles such leaders have to fight behind closed doors.

As leaders, you have committed to battling various types of conflict that will come your way. What's more, you not only commit to battling the conflict, but to keep your peace when all hell breaks loose. It takes a strong will and strong mindset to deal with the issues that always seem to find leaders. It can be very tough on a leader at times because he or she has to make decisions in a quiet room. Not everyone will be able to assist in the crucial decisions that have to be made in the midst of conflict. It's a difficult state of mind to be in when it's you who has to make the decision alone. Some people may think that leadership is a glamorous position to be in, but they must don't realize that heavy is the head that wears the crown.

CHAPTER 10

The Trials and Tribulations of Leadership

The Body

The weight of the crown of leadership can have an effect on your mind, body, and spirit at times. There will be plenty of late-night planning and issues so weighty that you may lose sleep. The position of leadership has no closing time and will steal your recommended eight hours of sleep right out from under you.

However, it is important that you do get an adequate amount of rest; otherwise, you won't be able to function at your optimal best. Personally, I am a firm believer in power naps. These brief moments of rest during the day get me so rejuvenated! I wake up ready to take on the world again.

Leaders are pulled in so many directions at times that it's easy to lose balance. It happens because even though we are superheroes, we are still human. And as humans, we still owe our minds and bodies what they crave . . . *rest!*

Some leaders suffer badly because they may come into their leadership role with a health issue, and the pressures that come with the position can put their health at high risk. It's a huge decision to make to decide to stay in a leadership position even though it could make your health issue worse . . . or even deadly. We've all seen leaders have heart attacks, strokes, pass out, or even just not eat properly. Sometimes the leadership position can be the worst decision for your health even though you have the best intentions in mind. Keep in mind that you can't be a true leader if you can't make hard decisions to improve lives—including valuing your own life and health.

The Mind

I need to be honest with you. In your leadership position, if you do not have a strong mind, you will lose your mind. This is not a statement to take lightly, as it can be damaging to your business and personal life to lose yourself in this way. As powerful as the mind is, it is simultaneously quite delicate—sometimes even fragile. We cultivate thoughts, make decisions, and move our body parts all with our minds. If we lose our mind, our sense of life is lost.

To deal with the stresses that come with leadership, you must cultivate a strong mind. Leaders come into contact with all types of people. This also means there will be several types of opinions for you to handle on a daily basis. As a leader, you automatically make yourself susceptible to public opinion. Sure, there will be public praise, but there will also be public ridicule from people who want to humiliate you. Oftentimes, as your leadership role grows, your personal life may be dragged into spotlight.

It is of the utmost important to unplug every now and again from your position in order to maintain your sanity. You have to be able to remember who you are outside of leading the masses. Without these moments, it will be easy for you to forget why and how you came to be a leader in the first place. Meditation and classical music are my means of unplugging from the daily activities and interactions of my role. You must make time for yourself if you want to be an effective leader. A great leader will find the time to drop everything so that they can hold it together. The mind is everything. If it is lost, you are lost.

The Spirit

The reality of being a leader is that it can be quite easy for people (including you) to forget that we are human—humans with human emotions and problems, such as shortcomings, bouts of low self-esteem, and disappointment. If you haven't already, you will encounter some very dark moments. These moments will happen in your professional as well as your personal life. When these moments arise, there's no telling who, if anyone, will be around to help you see the light at the end of tunnel. It is in these moments that you must take power over yourself and tap into your spirit.

> *"The wind blows the hardest the closer you get to the mountaintop."*
>
> —Daredevil, Episode #12

The universe allows for the spirit to be tested in the moments of trial and tribulation. It is its way of forcing you to make the decision of whether you are strong enough to hold your title. I am a man of prayer and persistence. It is part of my belief system that dark moments arise to strengthen my will and passion to be great in the world. Leaders must recognize these moments, because as you lead people into uncharted lands, your spirit will be tested. You will be tested over and over; with each test seeming harder than the last. It will beat you up and make you question your ability to lead. During your moments of peace (such as meditation, prayer, resting, eating, driving, reading the newspaper, etc.), take a moment to cultivate the spirit of your inner warrior. You know your mission. You are here to serve in the highest capacity possible. It takes guts, a strong desire, and a strong mind to lead effectively and with an unwavering spirit.

The Relationships

Balancing your relationships should be one of your top priorities when in a leadership role. Sometimes you may even have to release a few relationships in order to maintain your balance. You may not want to, but when you have responsibilities, you also have the responsibility to allocate your time wisely. It is simply not possible to have a true relationship with everyone you encounter. Some relationships create heavy baggage and that is not what you should be carrying. Remember, in order to have a relationship, you have to RELATE. If there is little to no relation happening, it may be time to let that connection go and make room for others. As you grow in your position as a leader, you may also grow out of a few relationships with people.

The fact of the matter is, you won't be liked by everyone; sometimes even the people you lead will turn their backs on you. Some of the people you thought would be alongside you during your leadership term may become jealous, causing a distance to arise between you. Family and friends may never understand the full capacity of your work and wonder why you aren't around like you used to be. Ralph Waldo Emerson said, "Whatever course you decide upon, there is always someone to tell you that you are wrong." People may try to deter you from your purpose and when you don't fall in line, they may turn their backs on you. If you've had a difficult time with this, bear in mind that it is an unfortunate experience that all leaders have to endure. You are in good company.

Do an inventory check. (Have you read my previous book *Skyscraper*? I discuss the importance of ritually doing inventory checks on yourself to ensure you stay on the right path.) I always suggest that my mentees have a sit-down with a close friend and/or family member(s) when they take their first leadership roles. Let them know that things may change and that your time may be allocated more to your leadership role from now on. Communication is key. I'm not saying this will work without fail, but it can at least give them some insight of where your mind is, instead of taking the changes as a personal attack.

Please understand: even with all your suggestions and warnings, even with the clearest communication, you will never be able to please everyone. Some may feel that you've left them behind and others may feel like you owe them your entire life. You may have to deal with gossip originating from those you felt could trust. You may have to endure tear-filled conversations with those who feel hurt by your personal decisions. Remember, when you have a mission to lead and it's part of the bigger plan of your life, no one can stop it from happening. Just be thankful for each person who has come into your life and remember that everyone comes into your life for a reason and season.

Learning to Move Forward from Failure

I titled this chapter "Who Saves the Superhero" because people forget that leaders need help just as much as they do. Who prays for the pastor when he or she needs it? Who advises the coaches of professional sports teams? Who advises the president and prime ministers? Leaders have family and friends that they care deeply about. What happens when they lose one of those individuals in the midst of leading? When they are dealing with personal issues just like everyone else, who do they confide in who will have their best interests at heart?

These are real questions to ask because leaders are real people, too. We, as leaders, don't always make the right decisions, although it may seem right at the time. Failure comes eventually and it can prove hard to move forward afterward. It is important to be a person of resilience and determination even when you feel like you've had the wind knocked out of you. It takes great courage to get back in the ring after taking a huge beating from an opponent. This is an important trait to have. As leaders, we know that our biggest opponent is none other than ourselves. So prove your "beaten-up" self wrong. Stand up. Dust yourself off. Get back in that ring.

Sometimes it's helpful to remember that all great leaders have had their share of knockdowns. There were times they had to claw themselves back into the ring to go another round at leading a business, community, people, or country. Greatness is not developed on an easy trail. The best among us developed through applied knowledge, better known as experience. Don't dwell on your failure or hardship; refer to it when the need arises. Learn to look at failure as a learning experience. Use it to share with others going through a similar moment. Let's "fail" our way to success!

The Man in the Arena

"It is not the critic who counts; not the man who points out how the strong man stumbles, or where the doer of deeds could have done them better. The credit belongs to the man who is actually in the arena, whose face is marred by dust and sweat and blood; who strives valiantly; who errs, who comes short again and again, because there is no effort without error and shortcoming. But who does actually strive to do the deeds; who knows great enthusiasms, the great devotions; who spends himself in a worthy cause; who at the best knows in the end the triumph of high achievement, and who at the worst, if he fails, at least fails while daring greatly, so that his place shall never be with those cold and timid souls who neither know victory nor defeat."

—Theodore Roosevelt

CHAPTER 11

The Reinvention of Yourself

The famous American painter, Bob Ross, hosted a television show in the 1980s on the PBS network. Each episode started with his signature soft and warm greeting that all the viewers loved. He would then talk about what he would be painting and get everyone excited to follow along in their homes so that they could duplicate what they saw Bob create on television.

During one of his shows, Ross said, "There are no mistakes. You can fix anything that happens." I believe this concept fits perfectly with this chapter. We have a lot of fear when we first touch a blank canvas. But once we get over that fear, that's when we really experience and get to enjoy painting our vision. Apply this to the reinvention of yourself when the time has come for you to change with your seasons.

Reinvention means to invent again or make anew, especially without knowing that the invention already exists. But it also means to remake or make over, as in a different form. We will always have to rise to certain situations to show or prove our leadership. There will be responsibilities that we have to be prepared to accept. To be adaptable enough to be able to reinvent yourself in order to take on those responsibilities helps makes a great leader.

Be Honest with You about You

When making the decision to reinvent yourself, you must first be honest with yourself. There are going to be sacrifices you have to make and issues you need to resolve in the process of making an entirely new you. You will need to be honest with yourself about your strengths and weaknesses. You will need to have a clear understanding of what areas need transformation so that you can be a dynamic and effective leader. There is no way around this first step. If you don't have an honest and clear understanding of your current self, how will you be able to create your new and improved self?

> "*Mastering others is strength.*
> *Mastering yourself is true power.*"
>
> —Lao Tzu

Create a Support System

After you have a heart-to-heart conversation with yourself, you can begin to reach out to those who you feel will be a great support to you during your process of self-reinvention. To your benefit, you are now fully aware of your strengths as well as your weaknesses. Share these with your support system so that when your weaknesses show up, you are able to reach out to them for help. They can be your encouragement when dealing with your weak areas.

Make sure you have mentors in place so that you can contact them when the need for advice and wisdom arises. You should not have to rely on them all the time, but at the very least, they will be available to make sure you are on the right path and/or give you a necessary push. They are your elders in the village. They are your angels, who are making sure that your own wings are strong enough to take flight to new heights.

This process of self-reinvention is no easy task. You are becoming someone new, which means you will have to experience new things. Be supreme in your process, but take your time so that you receive everything that will make your inner glow shine through to the outside.

Visualize the End First

Once you have a solid support system in place, the next step is to visualize the end of your metamorphosis. After you have gone through the process, what do you expect from yourself? How do you want to talk, walk, and interact with others? How will your leadership style change? What are the words that will describe the new you? You must have these target words imprinted in your mind prior to taking the next step because they will be your inner compasses to make sure you know why you are doing this.

After you visualize who you want to become and how you will lead, then you can begin to evaluate your current situation. You must sit by yourself, analyze the knowledge you've received, and conduct your own investigation. Make a thorough evaluation of your character, environment, leadership skills, and your current ability to lead. There may be some areas that don't need an uplift or a change, but that doesn't mean there aren't others that need updating. Once you have a clear view of what you are pushing to become, you will surely recognize what you need to work on to create a new you.

> *"When you want to reinvent yourself, you must be willing to sacrifice good for greatness later."*

Radical Change Takes Radical Faith

The future isn't promised to anyone, but we have faith that we will see it. As you sacrifice today's self to become the you that you want to see tomorrow, you are going to have to do some things that no one will expect from you. You are going to have to believe in yourself more when others don't. You are going to have to push yourself more when others won't. You may have the strongest safety net imaginable of people in your circle, but they can't see the vision as you do. You were born with the vision to become better so that you can do better for others. Radical faith is what you are going to need to achieve this. Your faith and actions for transformation will have to be beyond ordinary and higher than extraordinary.

If you really want to be the best you, you are going to have to set your old belief system on fire and build a new and improved one. You are going to have to find the strength to cultivate unwavering courage when not everyone around you agrees with your belief system. You must be more determined than your current self, even if those around you think your self-reinvention is pointless.

You are going to have to set the bridge on fire and know that there is no going back to the old you. Your values and belief system are the heartbeat to the change you want to see in and outside of yourself. Think of it this way: moving into a new place on a poverty-stricken street doesn't mean you've made it out of your situation. You have to change it *all* to become the better version of you.

As a leader, you will lead through image, language, and mindset. Those who follow you do so because you represent their collective vision of change. They follow your language because you speak in theirs. They follow your image because you look like what they believe could be a reality for them. When you reinvent yourself as who you yearn to be as a leader, you will attract the people who share a common thread of what's within you. It's never about you, it's about who you relate to.

Let Truth Settle In

An interview I saw with Matthew McConaughey during the year he won his first Oscar went deep into his past, explaining how he rose to great success in the acting world. I was struck by a few lines he spoke about his industry dry spells and when he started gaining massive success.

During the time that he began to rise high in his celebrity status, McConaughey fled to South America for a month. No one really knew him and he didn't speak the native language. This gave him the opportunity to detach and regroup just as his fame began to blossom; he believed that what he did was very good for him. "You have to get to a place where our memory can catch up with us; where the truth can settle," McConaughey said. He explained that success and popularity could become unbalancing. It is important that we are always able to locate our center, our balance.

This type of mentality should be constantly applied. When you do well in anything, you will receive recognition and popularity in some shape or form. But we must do an inventory check on ourselves so that we don't lose sight of what really matters. It is important that we find time to disconnect and reflect when necessary. Popularity is the deadliest of drugs to the ego. Make sure you don't overdose on success.

You are a leader. You don't ever want to be in a state of confusion or lack of confidence because you didn't take the time to detach and reflect. I always say that the most powerful people on earth are the individuals who can cultivate peace in the middle of chaos. To be a leader such as this, you must detach, reflect, cultivate, and lead with confidence and unwavering faith.

CHAPTER 12

Mastering Leadership at the Highest Level

In my previous book *Skyscraper*, I introduced my equation for creating a legacy of success: D3=F

Discipline x Dedication x Determination = Forever

In summary, it means that if you are able to fulfill these three areas with commitment, your name will last forever. You will become the person that others study to gain insight on how to perfect their own skill set and talent.

As I stated earlier, there are several characteristics that need to be acknowledged when a person is a considered a leader. But what does it take to be a true master of leadership? One of my favorite authors,

Robert Greene, wrote a fantastic book called *Mastery*. In the book, he discusses in great detail what it takes to be a master at anything. I want to share a few pointers that I think you should definitely take into consideration as you continue to lead.

Always Be Like a Child and Stay Curious

Leaders must forever remain curious about all that is around them in life. They must yearn for a better understanding of people, places, and things. When leaders have a childlike curiosity, they begin to see the depths of their missions. They push to break barriers and limits that may have been set by past leaders with old ways of thinking. When children are curious, they question everything. When leaders stay curious, they have the capability to master anything.

Use Your Imagination in its Entirety

Leaders must exercise their imaginations as much as possible. All that we have experienced in life thus far has been in connection to someone's use of their imagination. For example, you've been on an airplane because someone had the audacity to use their imagination and created this amazing apparatus that allows us to fly in the sky like birds. It is our duty as leaders to explore the world and see its glory for ourselves, while imagining what glories are yet possible.

Never Seek Comfort

If you are currently in a comfortable position that has allowed you to become complacent, you are going to have to let it go. Becoming a master in leadership takes a great deal of work and there will be unsettling moments during your development. You can't seek for something that you will never be able to enjoy. You don't want to merely be a leader; you want to be a *dynamic* leader who could never be held in comparison. Seek ways to become more resilient, confident, determined, strong, and bold as you lead others into the unknown. Let me offer a simple reminder to help keep your focus: To whom much is given, much is required.

Let Your Work Speak for You

There is nothing more devaluing of a leadership image, nor more aggravating, than the shouting of a self-proclaimed leader. True leaders don't have to advertise themselves. If you are doing the work that real leaders are supposed to do, then it will show and word will travel fast. It's best to keep your head down and focus on being effective at planning, strategic execution, and getting positive results from those you lead. Quality is always silently powerful.

Have a Sense of Purpose

You know your purpose. You know you were placed on this earth to be extraordinary. Your life has great meaning and you need to remind yourself of this during the good times and especially during the hard times. We assign value to whatever gives off a sense of value. Place value on yourself. Know that the decisions you make are in connection with your purpose. Take pride in the fact that you lead with purpose and you are living in your purpose. You are one of the most valuable players in this movement for a better world.

Commit to Apprenticeship

To be a master, you must learn from the masters. Every influential leader was under someone's wing during their time of development and change. As you gain momentum and develop various areas of your ability to lead, you will have to come to terms with change. You need to have someone who can take you under their wing so that you can get better acquainted with your new level of performance. Apprenticeships in the trades typically last between three and six years; base your learning on these patterns and use these years for great development, observation, and trial and error.

The Five Steps to Mastery

In his book, Robert Greene talked about his 12 years of studying high-level achievers and people of great power. During his research, he realized that most of the individuals who were of this high stature were not necessarily great students. Most of them came from poverty or broken homes, and their parents or siblings did not show any extraordinary abilities. These powerful leaders and high achievers simply had an intense desire to develop high-level skills and master their talent.

Step One: Discover Your Calling

We are all different. We all have a particular path that we must walk that no other person has ever walked before or will be able to walk for us. It is imperative that we take the necessary space and time to become curious about our lives and the decisions we are about to make for ourselves. I stated earlier that having a childlike curiosity is one of the attributes I strongly believe helps you to become a master of leadership. This also goes for finding meaning in your life.

Dealing with the first step, Greene stated, "You will find your calling by thinking back to your childhood, reflecting on these early interests that you may have strayed from."

Step Two: Apprentice with Intensity

In this phase of the process, you are seeking and confirming where you will get your most valuable education for the skill you want to master. The individuals and groups that take you under their wing will be considered the best for developing the skills you possess. It is also in this stage that you make the vital decision to go into the environments that have the best opportunities for improving you so that you can be the impactful leader you want to be tomorrow.

Greene gives a warning to those in this stage by saying, "The great danger in the beginning is the temptation to try to gain attention, to prove yourself before you are ready. Instead you must take a step back—your goal is to transform yourself into a consummate observer."

Once settled in this stage, you may become a serious student and begin learning all that you possibly can. Now you will begin to see yourself grow in the skills/talents you possess, as well as what you acquire. But be very clear that you must exit the environment when you have learned all that you can. You will have to move on from mentors that no longer can help you as you gain momentum and progress to the next level of learning and experiencing. This is normal in the process of development. What isn't normal is believing that once you become the big fish in the small pond, you don't have to swim in the ocean. If you are developing yourself to be a great leader, you are going to have to leave the environments you once knew so that you can continuously grow and make a larger impact with the skills and talents you possess.

Step Three: Gain Social Intelligence

Social intelligence is the ability to see a person in their most authentic light. It is in this stage that we usually try to make a person live up to the image or emotional state that we envision them to have (or want them to be).

Here are the two things Greene states about this:

- ★ "First, you must learn to read people in the moment, seeing them as individuals and trying to gain an understanding of them from the inside out.
- ★ "Secondly, you must also learn how to see yourself as others see you, using them as a mirror to help correct your own social flaws."

These skills are essential to the longevity of your success in your development process and your interaction with others as an impactful leader.

Step Four: Awaken Creative Energy

Robert Greene states, "After a lengthy apprenticeship, the counter-tendency is to become conservative with what you know, to follow the paths others have forged."

Leaders in this step will yearn to apply what they have been learning in the most creative way possible. During the apprenticeship process, our brains gained tons of information; we'll now be looking for ways to apply it in action. We have to be completely open to the world and let our creative juices flow. It is here that creative application is applauded.

Step Five: Develop High-Level Intuition

In this final step, we transcend all things in the area we have set out to master. If you take a look at any of the great leaders of the past, there were moments when they started to break away from what people viewed as ordinary. People began to *experience* them rather than *meet* them. Leaders become more than the sum of the parts they study. They begin to see beyond the basic state of learning and studying. They become the embodiment of what they studied.

As a leader with high-level intuition, you begin to see answers to problems before others, you are able to create plans that can affect the lives of future generations, and you begin to have more clarity on things that many others will never see.

Robert Greene stated, "All of us have access to this higher form of intelligence, one that can allow us to see more of the world, to anticipate trends, to respond with speed and accuracy to any circumstance. This intelligence is cultivated by deeply immersing ourselves in a field of study and staying true to our inclinations, no matter how unconventional our approach might seem to others."

With deep-rooted faith and a great deal of energy poured out during your time of leadership, there is no telling how impactful a leader you can truly be.

Abandon Yourself

Alexander the Great, the Greek king, once led his troops across a hot, arid desert. After nearly two weeks of marching, when he and his soldiers were near death from thirst, Alexander pushed ahead.

In the noonday sun, two of his scouts brought him what little water they were able to find. It barely filled a cup. Alexander's troops were shocked when he poured the water onto the burning sand.

The king said, "It is of no use for one to drink when many thirst."

Treating those who report to you as partners or associates will not work if it's only a scheme or a strategy. It must be a genuine heart-felt expression of the true value you place on them.

When we truly believe in the potential of people, they rarely disappoint us. That is one of the messages of Max DePree, in his perceptive book, *Leadership Is an Art*. He recommends becoming "abandoned to the strength of others—admitting that we cannot know or do everything."

CHAPTER 13

Travel the World Constantly

There is no way you can be a global leader if you haven't traveled the globe. Travel is essential to your continuous learning and development. You can pay plenty of money to get a degree or PhD in leadership, but it means nothing if you haven't gotten real experience.

Leaders are developed by experience and the knowledge they apply during various situations. Through travel, leaders learn the similarities and differences between cultures. They begin to understand how people interact with each other in their homelands and in foreign situations. Leaders who travel recognize that truth isn't in one location. They also come to understand how we affect each other even if we are in different countries. Traveling challenges everything you were taught in school and the knowledge that was passed down to you from others.

Professor Warren Bennis of the University of California stated in his book, *Becoming a Leader*, "Clearly, to become a true leader, one must know the world as well as one knows one's self." How much truer could his statement be? The more you know of the world and the people in it, the more you are able to nurture your influence and impact on the world. You have to fall in love with the world and humanity to understand them. You must respect this beautiful world we live in if you want it to respect you in turn.

Question and Assuming

Albert Einstein once said, "If I had an hour to solve a problem, I'd spend 55 minutes thinking about the problem and five minutes thinking about solutions." One of the main reasons that I am pushing you (and those who want to be global leaders) to travel constantly is because you need to find truth and collect facts. You cannot lead people or an organization based on theory. What makes the information you received from others and through your formal education factual? You can't simply lead without experiencing other cultures and going out on your own to do your own research.

When you don't spend time questioning the views and the information you've received over the years, you will make decisions based on assumption. Assuming how people think, live, and experience the world can be very dangerous. Making assumptions can be the key that opens up the door of ignorance and disrespect on your part. You have a responsibility to make decisions and lead people with the most accurate information possible.

Great global leaders understand that the individuals with the best information and advisors make the biggest impact. They also know that they must *always* be a inquisitive student by questioning everything. Nobody on Planet Earth knows everything. This is why it is your responsibility to travel: to learn and experience as much as you can. Become well-versed in various cultures. If you are going to make a global impact as a leader, make sure that you get all your facts straight and have first-hand experience to call upon.

The Road Is Always Under Construction

The journey of a leader is always under construction. This is because you are always evolving. You are constantly going to experience things that will test you, challenge you, and change you. Change is a part of life and we have to always repair damage or reconstruct areas in our lives so that we can be better prepared for whatever comes our way next.

Because our journey and position will always be under construction, it is best that we learn how to surrender and just be the best that we can be along the road. For example, when you are in a traffic jam, you can't do much about it. So you have to let go and do whatever you can, wherever you are. Some people play their favorite music, while others hold conference calls in the car. Some people take it as a moment to meditate, while others choose to be extremely angry due to the traffic. Leaders must be able to adapt in the most effective and positive way so they don't lose themselves on a road that will always be under construction.

Steering with Your Gut

The position of leadership will never be easy when you are making progress. (To be honest, it isn't easy even when no progress is made. It just feels worse.) As you begin to move forward and do your best to avoid the potholes and crazy drivers on your road, make sure you remember the order of these three gears the next time you head out on the road to effective global leadership:

- ★ Research
- ★ Strategy
- ★ Steer with Your Gut

Research the roads that you will take during the day, ensuring that you're choosing the ones that will enable you to be the most effective in your leadership no matter what problems arise. Take time to contact your support systems and look at all the possible opportunities that could benefit the people who follow you. Do in-depth research on the current issues that may arise and hinder your progress for the day. Begin to shift into Strategy mode.

Strategize your drive for the day. This is when you create your agenda and daily to-do list. This will always change throughout the day, but having a strategy in place is the preparation for success and positive impact. Success in leadership doesn't come by accident. It is intricately planned by the leaders who are confident and resilient enough to see it through. Strategy is the liberation of strength and genius from the leader. It involves foreseeing the finish line and crossing it before you've even taken your first step. Figuring out what the first step is can only be felt in the gut.

After all the research and strategy, actions have to take place. The first stirrings of action are only felt in the leader's gut after all the relevant information and options have been placed in front of them. We can have the best execution strategy but our gut has to be in agreement. Leaders do not have the luxury of second-guessing themselves when decision have to be made. They make the best decisions with the best information, which helps them make the proper decision from their gut.

When my mentors started to see my progress as a global leader, they always reminded me that my gut would never steer me wrong. That's where God talks to me when I need a higher sense of confirmation that I am making the right or wrong decision. My heart could be with the people, my head might be with my research and strategy, but my gut is where God's voice lies. If you don't believe me, ask anyone who's had to make a tough leadership decision on a high level. As a global leader, you have to make the final call, and when in doubt, trust your gut.

Change of Pace

Your pace will change constantly while on the leadership road. This is because things will always change and surprises will always jump out at you as you lead your people. As the world changes, so will your role as a leader. What is relevant today could be forgotten by tomorrow. When you embrace change, you are able to easily navigate into the future while many others will be left behind. Great leaders adapt in the best way they know how. They find the best pace for them and then they pick up speed to make the biggest impact they can.

CHAPTER 14

Leading Through Engagement

Being engaged with your followers, local community, global community, and leadership team is vital to the value and influence of your leadership. Many people believe that being seen as a leader is more than enough. But just being seen or sitting in an office all day strategizing does not make you effective or influential. All leaders are servants who have a weighty responsibility to serve their followers in the best possible manner. Being engaged will ensure your position at the top of the list when people talk about who has made a difference in their lives.

Local Community Engagement

No matter how influential you become in the world, never forget the local community in which you live. This also goes for the communities that surround you. Being engaged with local residents and understanding what is happening in your local community keeps you grounded. Create opportunities for the children in your community to get to know you. You can receive praise from all over the world for the changes you are making in foreign countries, but if you can't do the same for your own community, you may lose your safety net when you need it most. Remember, change starts at home.

Get to know your neighbors and make it a point to meet your community's leaders. I know that our time is very limited and we can't commit to too many things. But something as simple as hosting or attending a community event to show your support goes a long way. You can provide resources that your local community may not have. You are a global leader, and your local community is part of the global community you are serving. Make sure you leave a good impression within your community, because the people there are the ones who will watch over your house while you are away.

Global Community Engagement

Being engaged with communities to which you are connected around the world can be a tedious task at first. I suggest coming up with a simple and flexible structure that focuses on open communication with your global community. You can visit various countries, sure, but what about when you can't get there for a few months? How about when you can't make it to areas that need your help? How do you engage with them from a distance?

Global leaders have a responsibility to provide an open line of communication for their global community. This could involve maintaining an authentic dialog using social media platforms. It could be confirming one day each week to host a live chat online so that questions can be answered and connections can be strengthened. No matter the format, communication is key to how well you engage in the position of leadership.

When traveling abroad, I am always thinking of how I can leave my mark in that particular location. I am also thinking about how I can more strongly impact the individuals I will be meeting. I will spend hours listening and having conversations with locals. I make an effort to get to know more about the family, friends, hobbies, and favorite music of those within the global community that I serve.

The global community is enormous and your daily goal is to make the world seem more welcoming through consistent, open communication. Always remember this tip when you start gaining momentum: staying involved and engaging authentically is what gives true and great leaders longevity.

Leadership Team Engagement

You can't make the impact you would like to all by yourself. That is why it is crucial to establish a leadership team and constantly assist in their development. You can learn just as much from your team as they can learn from you. When you engage with them, you are creating an impact from within. You build loyalty and receive commitment through the intensity of their actions. Engagement is another way of giving attention to those you value, making them aware that you see them as valuable to the decisions at hand.

When it comes to your team, ask questions and allow them to be open with you. Getting their opinions and sharing their ideas with others is what engagement is all about. When you are creating a strategy, ask for your team's input so that everyone feels that they are part of the development process. Understand the needs of the individuals on your team. The issues within a person's private and professional lives do affect each other at times. Being engaged allows you to understand why a member of your team might be going beyond what is expected or not living up to their potential. Stay engaged with your leadership team and you will be able to have and attract the support that you will always need.

Inspire Fellow Leaders to Greatness

> *"To grow and be stretched, leaders of tomorrow must be given significant responsibility today."*
>
> —BILL GRAHAM, *THE LEADERSHIP SECRETS*

Align yourself with leaders who are making strides to make positive change in the world in their own way. Remember that everyone isn't cut from the same cloth, so you will have to be very cautious with whom you align yourself. While you are connecting with your fellow leaders of the world, find ways to help them when in need of support. Leaders, just like superheroes, must have allies along the way to keep them inspired and engaged. It's not easy to lead people into the future. It's not easy trying to balance your personal life with the life of a global leader.

Inspire your fellow leaders through your mentorship and advice when you see them walking into a situation you've been in before. Try to dig into your network and see if there is someone who would be a great connection for them. Leaders who share the same vision and passion to lead others don't feel intimidated or threatened by one another. Inspiration and motivation flourish when leaders connect with a similar vision. How great would it be to inspire someone by swapping stories?

Another great way to inspire or motivate your fellow leaders is by creating a mastermind group. This group would consist of leaders that you know all over the world. Once a month, hold a conference call where you each highlight experiences or things you've learned, allowing yourselves to be influenced by one another. Maintain open communication with your fellow leaders because they need you just as much as you need them.

The possibilities of how you might influence other leaders, or be influenced by them, can go beyond all you imagine. Everything that you represent and are connected to are other ways that leaders can be influenced and pushed to aim higher. Leaders can be influenced by the organization you lead, your leadership staff/team interaction with others, the image that is projected to the world, the culture you've established, or even how people engage with the vision you've set to accomplish together.

You have to be a leader of influence for all those around you. This includes positively influencing those who might even be in the same position as you.

INVICTUS

by William Ernest Henley

Out of the night that covers me,
Black as the pit from pole to pole,
I thank whatever gods may be
For my unconquerable soul.

In the fell clutch of circumstance
I have not winced nor cried aloud.
Under the bludgeonings of chance
My head is bloody, but unbowed.

Beyond this place of wrath and tears
Looms but the Horror of the shade,
And yet the menace of the years
Finds, and shall find me, unafraid.

It matters not how strait the gate,
How charged with punishments the scroll,
I am the master of my fate:
I am the captain of my soul.

CHAPTER 15

The Leadership of Mandela

> *"When the history of our times is written, will we be remembered as the generation that turned our backs in a moment of global crisis or will it be recorded that we did the right thing?"*
>
> —NELSON MANDELA

In the list of global leaders who have transcended in our lifetime, one name that will certainly be at the top of the list is Nelson Mandela. Nelson Mandela was 44 years old when he began his 27 years of imprisonment as a result of his drive to end apartheid in South Africa. He is remembered in high regard for his unrelenting pursuit of racial equality and his lifelong struggle against segregation and poverty, as well for his passionate belief in humanity. Following his release, he became the President of South Africa.

Mandela was a man of great pride, dignity, and self-respect. He always demanded the respect he believed he was due not just as a man, but more importantly, as a human being. He was the epitome of humility and transcending global leadership. I remember watching an interview with Mandela on the *Oprah Winfrey Show* years ago. She tried to persuade him into admitting that it was him who played the greatest role in the apartheid movement. He declined the notion that it was a solo act and began to give credit to all who he believed made this effort a reality. In fact, Oprah mentioned afterward that Mandela would not even allow the interview to continue until he was able to name as many contributors to this historical achievement as he could remember.

Mandela fought for respect and his dignity from the first day he stepped into the Robben Island prison. He instructed the prison guards to call him "Mr. Mandela." This would serve as constant reminder to the prison guards (as well as to himself) that although he was in prison, he would never be a prisoner. He knew that how you allow people to treat you determines how they respect you as a human being. He never showed any form of faltering in his beliefs or weakness in his intelligence. The audacity and courage he displayed to those who tried to suppress him speaks volumes about his character.

The Answers Are Hidden in the Youth

During an interview with Australian radio personality Neil Mitchell, Mandela was asked if children were his inspiration. Mandela replied, "Every human being, young and old, is an inspiration to those who want solutions to problems national and international; you can get a lot by listening carefully to what they say, sharing with them intimate feelings." He then went on to say, "Children are the most important assets in any country. Any country that does not care for its children is not worthy to be called a country."

As leaders, we must never forget the children of the communities we serve. Our entire future depends on it. If we have the capacity to go off into foreign lands and help in youth development, then we must do so. If we own or manage businesses, we must provide opportunities for the youth to learn responsibility and help to create positive change in our world. Children are innocent, unscathed by life's trials, and have been said to be the closest ear from God's mouth. It is this next generation that will either pick up or drop the torch we currently have in hand. It is up to us to teach them how to hold it and why it's important to carry it into the future.

I adore the beauty of a child's spirit. Children are the blank canvas we paint our wisdom on. They hold their tongues for no one and will truly give their love to those who give them the attention they need. What do you think happens when a country adores and loves the children of its land? A fruitful evolution. A country that adores all of its children will see prosperity for generations and generations to come.

Mandela's Optimism

> *"To spend 27 years at the prime of your life is a tragedy. And I regret those years that I have wasted in prison. But there are very positive aspects to it, too, because I had the opportunity to think about problems and reflect on my mistakes. I also had the opportunity to read very widely, especially biographies. And I could see that men, sometimes from very humble beginnings, were able to lift themselves with their boot strings and become international figures."*
>
> —Nelson Mandela, 1990

Through Mandela's statement, you can see and feel how he kept a positive perspective on the storms he had to endure for many years. Notice how he regarded being in prison as an "opportunity" to think, reflect, and broaden his horizons. Leaders, even in the early stages of their lives, are often known to have exercised resilience and optimism on life in general. Their views are usually very different than those of ordinary people. They always keep a positive outlook on any given situation.

> *"I am fundamentally an optimist. Whether that comes from nature or nurture, I cannot say. Part of being optimistic is keeping one's head pointed toward the sun, one's feet moving forward. There were many dark moments when my faith in humanity was sorely tested, but I would not and could not give myself up to despair. That way lies defeat and death."*
>
> —Long Walk to Freedom: The Autobiography of Nelson Mandela

Mandela's Leadership

"You have a limited time to stay on earth. You must try and use that period

for the purpose of transforming your country into what you desire it to be."

—Nelson Mandela,
Oprah Winfrey Show interview

The majority of people will agree that Nelson Mandela's leadership was something to be admired. He devoted his life to the vision of changing his country for the betterment of all people in that land. For this, he was bombarded with extreme resistance for wanting the change that was necessary for people to live in peace. He showed immense patience, faith, clarity in his vision, and the intelligence of a global leader. Just like every person that walks this earth, Mandela wasn't perfect, nor did he ever claim to be. But he definitely fulfilled his leadership role in an admirable manner that could not be fulfilled by anyone else.

In his autobiography *Long Walk to Freedom*, Mandela talks about how a leader "is like a shepherd. He stays behind the flock, letting the most nimble go out ahead, whereupon the others follow, not realizing that all along they are being directed from behind." What is so very interesting about that statement is that we know that Mandela really lived by what he preached. He went to the front lines when there were issues that needed to be hashed out. But when victories were won, he stepped back and let others celebrate in the front, in the spotlight. He said, "It is better to lead from behind and to put others in front, especially when you celebrate victory when nice things occur. You take the front line when there is danger. Then people will appreciate your leadership."

Mandela's Thoughts on Society

> *"It can be said that there are four basic and primary things that the mass of people in a society wish for: to live in a safe environment, to be able to work and provide for themselves, to have access to good public health, and to have sound educational opportunities for their children."*
>
> —Speech at the opening of the Oprah Winfrey Leadership Academy, January 2, 2007

At the beginning of this book, I stated that it is our responsibility to help establish and elevate the well-being of others. This view is very similar to what Mandela stated at the opening of the Leadership Academy in 2007. Leaders should be well informed and hands-on in the development process in order to make people in society more joyous and better off in their lives. It is just as important for leaders to create various outlets and platforms for healthy communication. In doing so, people are well-equipped with the necessary information to help sustain a positive and healthy state of being.

Mandela and Perseverance

While in prison, Mandela wrote a letter stating, "Difficulties break some men but make others. No axe is sharp enough to cut the soul of a sinner who keeps on trying, one armed with the hope that he will rise even in the end." Perseverance, by definition, means steadfastness in doing something in spite of difficulty or delay in achieving success. No matter the level of the leader, there will always be opportunity to activate perseverance. Many of us have exercised this ability in our earlier life stages in some capacity. For instance, I exercised it when I wanted to get out of the toxic environments I was being raised in as a youth. When you are acquainted with perseverance, you can go well beyond the limits that people try to put on you. You are able to seek and find an inner power that pushes you when all seems lost.

Mandela said, "I have walked that long road to freedom. I have tried not to falter; I have made missteps along the way. But I have discovered the secret that after climbing a great hill, one only finds that there are many more hills to climb. I have taken a moment here to rest, to steal a view of the glorious vista that surrounds me, to look back on the distance I have come."

Mandela on Peace

No matter what you become or pursue in life, there will always be people who feel they know what is best for you. As a leader, you will have individuals and groups who will try to deter you from making progress—even if what you stand for is for a positive impact on your local and global community. We have to pick our battles carefully when we are leading with a great vision for the future. One of the most important goals should be peace, especially when opposition comes your way. What I mean by peace is earning the respect and loyalty of those who try to hinder you and the people you lead.

Mandela said, "If you want to make peace with your enemy, you have to work with your enemy. Then he becomes your partner." I believe that you have to be open to cultivating a positive partnership with individuals or groups that may have tried to hinder your progress. That's what being a great global leader is all about: being able to do what the majority probably won't do because of ego, pride, or fear of what others may say. We are supposed to be peace cultivators and peacekeepers. If we never take the time to try and find ways to create partnerships of peace with those on the opposite side, we aren't leading in the best light given to us.

Mandela on Hate and Love

My generation has been making strides to change many of the old ideologies and mindsets of the past that were negative about people of different backgrounds. We live on the same planet, under the same sun, view the same moon, and wish upon the same stars. As leaders, it is our God-given duty to lead authentically and have transcending love for the entire global family. We all have our differences, but respect for our fellow man and woman must always be there. You have to lead with vision, integrity, passion, and transparency—and love. That is the energy source of all your actions and speeches.

> *"No one is born hating another person because of the color of his skin, or his background, or his religion. People*

must learn to hate, and if they can learn to hate, they can be taught to love, for love comes more naturally to the human heart than its opposite."

—Nelson Mandela

CHAPTER 16

The Mindset of Elon

It's been said that Elon Musk is our real-life Iron Man, the Tony Stark of our world. Elon is a South African-born, Canadian-American business magnate, engineer, inventor, and investor. He is the founder, CEO, and CTO of SpaceX; co-founder, CEO, and product architect of Tesla Motors; and chairman of SolarCity, as well as co-chairman of OpenAI. He is also a co-founder of Zip2 and PayPal.

Musk's businesses are purpose-driven rather than profit-driven businesses. Over the years, we've seen so many people cross over to the "Dark Side" because they believe that money is all that matters in business. But statistics show that businesses that are purpose-driven are more likely to stand the test of time and become more profitable. I wanted to highlight some of Musk's great advice here because he is a fellow entrepreneur and a leader in his own right. He has seen and experienced the things that separate him from the pack so that he can lead the pack.

Risk the Odds

Musk has stated, "When something is important enough, you do it even if the odds are not in your favor." Anything of great importance to you or others will come at a great cost. Many times as entrepreneurs and leaders, we can be faced with enormous backlash for chasing what seems impossible to the average person. We hear the word **"NO"** more than we hear **"I love you," "YES,"** or even **"That's a great idea."** Changing the world for the better is not going to sit well with people who are uncomfortable with being affected in their wallets or place of *complacency*. No one really wants to give up the empty seat next to them on the bus. That's why they always put something there, hoping you pass by—all because they don't want to be bothered or help someone be just as comfortable as them.

Entrepreneurship comes with longer odds than the lottery, but people still choose to take part in it—all with the hop that their luck will hit and turn whatever they are working on into a major success. I laughed when I heard Musk say,

"Being an entrepreneur is like eating glass and staring into the abyss of death." Even though that sounds quite harsh, it's a fact that entrepreneurs have it rough, especially when you are a purpose-driven entrepreneur. But I think he would agree with me when I say that if what we are pursuing is of great importance, we'll always be the first in line to give it a try.

Purpose-Driven Business Leader

Elon Musk realized early that he wanted to help change the world. That clarity and vision became the foundations for all that he has created. The same spirit has been shared in all of the companies and projects he has founded. Musk said,

> *"Going from PayPal, I thought: 'Well, what are some of the other problems that are likely to most affect the future of humanity?' Not from the perspective, 'What's the best way to make money?'"*

We live in a time where we must take great care of each other and the environment if we really want our next generation to enjoy a life better than we do now. So it is important to make sure your business is created and managed with a great spirit. Trust me when I say that nothing lasts long if it is coupled with a selfish purpose. It will destroy itself and/or all that it is connected to.

Talent Beats Numbers

Quality over quantity. It is always best to have talented people on your team, staff, and circle. You should always seek out the best talents because they will help you build the best net to catch the best opportunities. Even when you have problems that need to be solved, having the best people on your team can help you solve it in the best manner possible. Musk stated, "It is a mistake to hire huge numbers of people to get a complicated job done. Numbers will never compensate for talent in getting the right answer—two people who don't know something are no better than one—will tend to slow down progress, and will make the task incredibly expensive."

Along with talent, you need to be aware of the type of character a person possesses before you decide to put them in your circle to assist you in your leadership rol. Personality should be more important than profit when forming, managing, and leading a business.

Personality should alsobe an important focus when you are forming a team of people to help you be an effective global leader. It will save you headaches and heartbreaks to have people with great personalities on your side. Would you really want to deal with a talented but very inhuman person for a long period of time? On that topic, Musk said, "My biggest mistake is probably weighing too much on someone's talent and not someone's personality. I think it matters whether someone has a good heart."

Take Advantage of Your Opportunities

I always tell the entrepreneurs and global leaders that I advise to take advantage of what others take for granted. Many people wait on luck or for opportunities to drop into their lap. It is better to create your own luck and attract opportunities based on your work ethic. Musk stated, "If you go back a few hundred years, what we take for granted today would seem like magic—being able to talk to people over long distances, to transmit images, flying, accessing vast amounts of data like an oracle. These are all things that would have been considered magic a few hundred years ago."

We are well beyond the lifestyle of past generations and we must not let what we have today make us lackadaisical. What we have today was created by individuals who worked their entire lives to make this a reality for us. They worked relentlessly and sacrificed mediocrity for extraordinary. Let's make magic today!

Aim to Always Do Better

I am a leader who is always aiming to lead people better than I did yesterday. I am also an entrepreneur who aims to constantly enhance my businesses and products for my clients and customers. We should always question ourselves to see what we can do better. How can we give our best selves in situations and to others? Musk stated, "I think it's very important to have a feedback loop, where you're constantly thinking about what you've done and how you could be doing it better. I think that's the single best piece of advice: constantly think about how you could be doing things better and questioning yourself."

Invest in Yourself and Your Dreams

> *"I always invest my own money in the companies that I create. I don't believe in the whole thing of just using*

other people's money. I don't think that's right. I'm not going to ask other people to invest in something if I'm not prepared to do so myself."

—Elon Musk

If you believe in something, you won't wait for someone to jump in to start the car engine. You are going get in yourself, warm it up, and then pull off. If someone is willing to come along for the ride, then the door will be open for them. You have to invest in yourself and your dreams first because people are looking to see if you are passionate about what you are doing. Can you imagine a leader who is not passionate about the people they lead?

If you are taking the lead in building a company, believe me, you will have to invest your own money first. If you are taking the lead in building a better future for humanity, you'd best believe it will be your time and money being spent to prove to others how serious you are. Investing in yourself should feel good and be highly respected by others because it shows the faith you have in yourself and all you stand for.

Prepare for the Best

"You want to have a future where you're expecting things to be better, not one where you're expecting things to be worse."

—Elon Musk

I grew up hearing, "Always prepare for the worst," and "Save for a rainy day." But as an adult, I found this train of thought to be counterproductive. Why should we prepare for the worst when we are aiming for success? We should be preparing for the best results. We should be preparing to pass the tests. We should be saving for the moment to celebrate the lives we've saved and changed. The future belongs to those who see the world differently, even if those around them don't see it. Your success will be evident, because when you don't lead like everyone else, you don't end up like everyone else.

In college, Musk would often ask himself what would affect the future in a very positive way. This was his way of preparing for a brighter future. He was already questioning himself about how to create a better future. He was honest and purpose-driven, which helped him prepare for the best results of all his hard work. He would spend 100-hour weeks working on his businesses, which he did that so that he could receive the best outcome and not endure the worst-case scenario. We have great goals and visions in the position we currently hold. And we must remind ourselves that we are working hard to impact the world in the best way we know how. We don't have time to think about the what-ifs of negativity.

CHAPTER 17

The Opportunity of Having the Privilege

For almost two years, I've attended a small, private gym. Most of the time, when I arrive at the gym, an older woman with a warm smile greets me. It's the type of thing that anyone would love to receive before working out to preserve their focus. Going into the second year of my membership, the beautiful woman who always greets me told me that her son had decided to quit his job as a lawyer in New York to travel the world for a year. She explained to me how nervous and frightened she was for her son.

In my mind, I knew that he was about to be taken to another level. I knew that he was going to experience some things that many of his peers may never get a chance to. The reason I knew this is because he made a decision to follow what he felt in his gut. He decided to jump off the cliff to see how strong his wings were. I felt an amazing energy listening as his mother began to talk about the things her son was experiencing. It was evident that she was going along with him, in spirit, on his journey.

When he began his journey, the son decided to publish pictures of the places he stayed. He traveled throughout distant foreign lands, exploring India on his journey. Some of the places he visited were unbelievable. One day, before I left the gym, his mother showed me a picture that he'd posted on Instagram before he left India to head to his next location.

Under his picture, he described how a temple he visited fed close to 100,000 people daily. He talked about waiting in line for the "privilege" of washing their dishes. I was totally blown away by his statement. There is a beautiful energy that surrounds a person who looks at helping and humbling themselves for the serving of others as a privilege.

Privilege means a special right, an advantage, or immunity granted or available only to a particular person or group of people. During our journey of becoming who we were placed on this earth to be (in this case, a global leader), we will have many opportunities to have the privilege of doing something honorable for others. Global leaders must always look at life in this way: that we are servant entrepreneurs who have the privilege to benefit others.

CHAPTER 18

Handle Your Habits

None of us are exempt from having good and bad habits. Habits that hinder us from doing our best or leading effectively are considered bad habits. You may have some habits that were once permissible until you reached a certain age or position. Then things had to be changed as swiftly as possible. It may seem a little strange that I am talking about your personal habits in a leadership book, but let's be honest: your personal habits can and will affect your activities in public. I just want to make sure you don't slip and drop an opportunity because you never took the time to break your bad habits.

I've learned that we go through a transition every 90 days. (I speak about this more thoroughly in *Skyscraper*.) The little things we do absentmindedly on a daily basis create a positive or negative effect on us within a 90-day period. You are aiming to be a dynamic leader, so you have to sit and observe what you are doing every single day that may give you a negative outcome once the 90th day approaches.

Below are four highlights for you to remember and implement in your life so that you can break any bad habits still clinging on. You want to be as sharp as you possibly can. When you are out in the world helping people and developing communities, you don't want something to go wrong based on a small habit you never handled. Take these highlights seriously and watch your bad habits go away.

4 Ways To Handle Your Bad Habits

Highlight #1: Recognize, observe, and establish an understanding of your bad habit. You can't change anything until you first acknowledge it and know why it needs to be changed. There are always three actions to notice in your observations:

- ★ The Trigger: This is what causes you to do the bad habit
- ★ The Routine: This is what you automatically do once the habit has been triggered

- ★ The Reward: This is the feeling you receive from the habit

Highlight #2: Establish a new habit or new routine that will be used to override the current habit you are going to break. This routine must be consistent. You cannot switch up the routine because it is all about consistency. For 90 days, you must stick your new script.

Highlight #3: Reward yourself in the process. Make sure you cheer yourself on after every 30 days. This helps you to remain consistent and excited about establishing a new habit. Reminder: Yard by yard is hard, but inch-by-inch is a cinch. Celebrate every time you didn't fall into the ditch.

Highlight #4: No matter how hard it may get, never, ever quit. Getting rid of a habit you have gotten accustomed to is not easy. Just stay strong and steady. It will be well worth the effort in the long run. If you slip up a few times, don't stress too much abou it. Try again—just don't quit.

CHAPTER 19

Strategic Leadership

I am a strategic leader to the core. No one can convince me that developing strategy isn't important. In this section, I want to share with you insights about strategic leadership and the tools you'll need to be as effective as possible in this area. The various key points will specify the exact process and thought pattern to have when strategizing. Once you have a clear vision of what you want your outcome to be as a leader, you then move into developing a strategy of how to get to that outcome.

Strategic leadership is the **process** of using well-considered tactics and leadership styles to communicate a vision for an **organization**. It is also said to be one of the most effective ways to manage, motivate, and persuade staff to share in the same clear vision, and can be an important tool for implementing change or creating organizational structure within any group.

There are myriad styles of leadership—too many to list here. But within those, there are five leadership styles that I will briefly highlight so that you can pinpoint the style that is most beneficial to you and the ones you need to steer away from completely.

Authoritarian Style

This type of leader only focuses on a specific professional relationship. An Authoritarian leader believes that the secret to his or her success, longevity in legacy, productive environment, and growth in followers is direct supervision. The problem with this style of leadership is that the Authoritarian leader inadvertently forces his or her followers to support a vision even if it's not compatible with their own. These leaders place an intense focus on efficiency and look at every other style of leadership as a roadblock to progress.

Paternalistic Style

This type of leader acts as a parent by taking care of his or her team and staff like a parent. The Paternalistic leader shows complete concern for his or her followers or workers. In result, loyalty and trust are established between the leader, leadership team, and followers. Total commitment is expected from the entire team toward what this leader believes; they have no interest in doing something independently. There is a strong bond between the leader and their team due to this unmitigated loyalty. The trust is so strong that they rely on each other for support with problems and issues. This can be applied to personal or business situations alike. They believe in each other's advice and opinions and have a sense that any decisions will be in their best interest.

Democratic Style

This type of leader shares the decision-making capacity with his or her team members by promoting the team members' interests and by practicing social equality. The boundaries of democratic participation depend upon the organization's needs and the instrumental value of people's attributes (skills, attitudes, etc.). The Democratic leader leads with a style that holds that everyone, by virtue of their human status, should play a part in the group's decisions. This leadership style demands that the leader make decisions on who should be called upon within the group to take on tasks and who is given the right to make, participate in, and vote on decisions.

Laissez-Faire Style

In this type of leadership style, all the rights and power to make decisions are fully given to the individuals in an organization. This type of leader gives their team members and followers the complete freedom to make decisions concerning the completion of their work. These individuals are self-ruled while offering guidance and support when requested. The Laissez-Faire leader implements guided freedom, which provides their followers with all the materials necessary to accomplish their goals, but the leader does not directly participate in decision making unless the followers request their assistance.

Transactional Style

This type of leader motivates his or her followers through a system of rewards and/or punishments. This type of system is formed by contingent reward and management-by-exception. Contingent reward provides rewards, whether material or psychological, for effort shown and good performance. Management-by-exception allows the Transactional leader to maintain the status quo. The leader only gets involved when individuals in the organization do not meet the expected performance levels. The leader then takes the necessary actions to correct the behavior and improve performance. Such leaders also focus on increasing the efficiency of established routines and procedures. They believe it's most important to follow existing rules than to make changes to the organization.

When you are a leader with a Transactional style, you establish the standard practices that will help your organization in the following areas:

★ Maturity level

★ Goal-setting ability

★ Efficiency of operation

★ Productivity

Strive for Growth Through Strategic Leadership

Strategic leaders are the center and source for the professional education of their organizations' members.

They push to be inquisitive about the positive and negative experiences of other organizations that may have traveled the road they are currently on. These leaders are sharp at analyzing and applying the information they receive to make progress in their quest for positive results. Strategic leaders are constantly aware of how they approach problems and aim for growth. This leadership style can either hinder or accelerate the progress and impact of the entire organization. Leadership styles vary based upon the changes that the organization has to deal with from moment to moment. Change is always the revolving door in front of a leader's eyes while their team/staff/followers stands behind, awaiting their turn. It takes dynamic skills and tools to formulate and implement the right strategy when dealing with change.

Change Management

Before we go into the process of strategic leadership, I must briefly talk about change management. That's because all strategic leaders must be able to stand strong by their strategy and in its presentation. Having a complete understanding of the approach before the plan is implemented is always your best move.

Change management refers to any approach to transitioning individuals using methods intended to redirect the use of resources, business process, budget allocations, or other modes of operation that significantly reshape a company or organization. When we talk about change management, we are talking about an approach that takes into full consideration the entire organization and the changes that are needed. The practices and principles that are created make change management a tool for change focused solely on the individual(s). Change management takes a direct focus on analyzing how your organizational groups and connected individuals are affected by the transition at hand.

The Need for Change Management and Models

Change management is a necessity, especially for global leaders. It handles the constant international integration of global views, innovative new products, new ideas, and various cultural dynamics. We're living in a time where technology is constantly and comprehensively evolving. For these reasons, the environments in which global leaders are embedded keep changing.

For current generations, social media is heavily utilized for communication, consuming news, conducting research, etc. There is no denying that social media and mobile adaptability have revolutionized our modern environments, particularly where organizations and their business structures are concerned. This in itself is a major cause for an increased need for change management, because this revolution is accompanied by an increase in the availability and accountability of knowledge. This may or may not be considered a good thing.

Too much easy access to anything can be cause for concern. There is an overload of information that is released through technology and there is no real way to determine its validity. As a result, leaders of organizations and businesses make horrible decisions based on bad information, leading their teams, customers, and followers down the wrong path due to wrong data taken from these social media and mobile outlets.

Thus, it's vital that leaders utilize change management to retrieve the most accurate information. The strategic leadership approach must be equipped with the right data in order to allow the organization to transition into the new vision.

When trying to determine which model, strategy, or technique to implement during the change management process as a strategic leader, you must adhere to these four factors:

1. Levels, goals, and strategies
2. Measurement system

3. Sequence of steps

4. Implementation and organizational changes

In 1996, Dr. John P. Kotter, a professor at Harvard University, published a book entitled *Leading Change*. In the book, he shared his thoughts on leadership and presented his Eight-Step Process for Change Management. I love these steps and have been using them successfully in my position as a global leader. I have provided his steps here for you to use at will.

John Kotter's Eight-Step Process for Leading Change

1. Establish a Sense of Urgency

    - Create opportunity for those within your organization that will get them excited to achieve the goal(s) in short amount of time.

    - Be very clear with examples to why urgent change is necessary.

    - Identify potential, and current crisis, that need to be defused.

2. Create the Guiding Coalition

- [ ] Establish a group of individuals who have the influence and power to make the change you are seeking.

- [ ] Attract the most effective leaders for the process by showing enthusiasm and passion for the vision.

- [ ] Continuously invest time and energy to making sure your group can work effectively with each other.

3. Develop a Vision and Strategy

    - [ ] Establish a clear vision that will assist in directing the efforts for change.

    - [ ] Spend quality time developing strategies that will help you achieve the vision for change.

4. Communicate the Change Vision

    - [ ] Use every opportunity and resource to describe the vision and strategies.

    - [ ] Keep all communication as simple as possible.

    - [ ] Establish partnerships and keep the vision attractive through storytelling.

- [ ] Establish new behaviors and results through the group you established when you have to explain the urgency of implementing change.

5. Empower Employees for Broad-Based Action

    - [ ] Establish a structure or protocol that continuously checks for obstacles that could hinder the group from effectively achieving the vision.

    - [ ] The group will be able to move towards the vision smoothly if you are able to constantly show active participation of identifying and removing obstacles (i.e. people, situations, plans).

    - [ ] Reward individuals for making specific change during the process.

6. Generate Short-Term Wins

    - [ ] Create short-term goals that will help the group achieve the long-term goals.

    - [ ] The enthusiasm within the group will enhance due to continuous small achievements. These short-term goals must give little room for failure.

- ☐ Thoroughly analyze these short-term goals to make sure the investment of time, energy and money will be worth it. Each target short-term goal must be justified.

7. Consolidate Gains and Produce More Change

    - ☐ Change after each achieved goal and reflect on the pros / cons (See PPC evaluation).

    - ☐ Establishing new short-term goals that can help build the momentum of the last achieved goal.

    - ☐ Introduce new change agents and leaders to the team when necessary. We must build on the momentum and change what is happening with positive momentum.

    - ☐ Don't declare the achievement of the vision too early. Keep improving your process, group, execution, and communication for greater change.

8. Anchor New Approaches in the Culture

    - ☐ Change must be part of the culture of your organization.

    - ☐ Group leaders must constantly speak of the vision of change.

☐ Highlight the success of the group due to the new behavior patterns that have been established.

☐ Create a plan that highlights individuals who leave the group but understands that their contribution will always be recognized and appreciated.

☐ Constantly show groups and new group members where change has happened to keep everyone excited and focus.

PDAC 4-Step Process

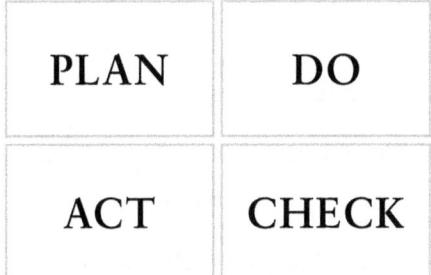

Another model you can use when dealing with change management is the Plan-Do-Check-Act Cycle (PDCA). It's a very simple and effective way of tackling problems, managing transitions, and guiding others in making the right decisions. This is a method businesses often use when focusing on improving products and processes.

Plan

- ☐ Establish objectives to deliver results that are aligned with target goal(s) and vision.

Do

- ☐ Work the plan that has been established, execute the process, and complete the task that was established. Afterwards, collect the data to analyze in your CHECK and ACT phases.

Check

- ☐ Study actual results.
- ☐ Compare against expected results to identify any differences.
- ☐ Convert data into information.
- ☐ Look for any deviation during the execution of the plan and also look for any positive moves made within the execution.

Act

- ☐ If you review the information in the CHECK step and it confirms that the PLAN strategy that was initiated in the DO step is an improvement over the prior standard (baseline), then that becomes the new standard (revised baseline) for how the organization should ACT moving forward.

- ☐ If you review the info in the CHECK step and it shows that the PLAN strategy that was initiated in the DO step is not an improvement, then the existing standard (baseline) will stay the same.

- ☐ No matter the outcome (positive or negative), if the CHECK step showed something that you never even expected, then there is some more learning to be done on your end, which will suggest potential future PDCA cycles.

CHAPTER 20

Balancing the Change Process

Various changes happen within organizations at any given time, so you will need to balance the process of changes you are making. Here is a four-step process for managing the change effectively:

1. Recognize the change(s)
2. Adjust to the company's needs
3. Train and develop the team for the needed change(s)
4. Gain the support of team members by making the appropriate adjustments

It's wise to research your current situations to understand exactly what needs to be changed. Make sure to specify the objectives, content, and process in your change management plan. You must also have an innovative way to communicate with your various audiences, as they will change periodically. Align your expectations with those of your team and your followers. Reminder: efficiency and leadership commitment are the keys to the overall success of the balancing act!

Many leaders tend to forget the true value of infrastructure in an organization and the value of leveraging change through technology. There has to be a synergy of alignment and integration between strategic, social, and technical components for a positive impact to sustain itself over the long term. This can only be true when you combine people who have valuable skill sets. This can prove to be a challenge in the area of organizational integration, combining the sum of various skills into an integral whole.

One of the very few constants in life is change. You, along with the team you develop, will have to be able to embrace flexibility. Change will constantly make success and achievement seem unattainable. Information will continually change and you will have to make sure the content and data you receive is as accurate as possible. This also means you will have to research to make sure your projects and goals can align themselves with the appropriate information for the relevant time period. This is usually a challenge for leaders to navigate. But if you can balance this along with the integration process, you will be just fine.

Strategic Leadership Process

Strategic leadership provides techniques that focus on the organization and its followers when making a decision about the best purposes and practices to remain relevant and impactful. Sustainability is a major concern in the strategic leadership process; it does no good to make a change this week that will be irrelevant the next. Additionally, the leader must show that he or she is able to adapt for the greater good of their followers. It is said that if a leader and his or her organization fail to adapt to changes (e.g., technology, climate, economic factors), then the organization becomes obsolete.

The Execution

The execution of a strategy, whether good or bad, is based on the information provided by you, the leader, or based upon the personal belief of your team/followers. When leaders provide a platform with a foundation based on very weak planning, it can leave decisions and actions very unclear for the team (or followers), who may have trouble following along.

Information is the most valuable tool for execution. If you have done your job to the best of your ability, meaning you have gathered the most accurate information available at the time, there shouldn't be any reason to second-guess yourself. You should be a person of great faith and strength. The information you receive flows freely through, and to, everyone who has lent their ear. This helps you meet the expectations of your followers and/or organization. You also meet expectations through strategic decisions and actions developed and executed in the most brilliant way you find possible. You can't succeed on your own; you must have a solid team, because you alone will not be able to learn, do, or create faster than the world is changing. You must bring in those who can leverage their skills in the areas where you're lacking. In conclusion, if you are able to adjust flexibly to the conditions that must be met, you will see great strides in your strategic leadership.

Leaders and Their Vocabulary

Much can be said about the manner in which a leader manages. Much can also be said about their belief system and how it affects the decisions they make each day. But vocabulary is another area that plays a significant role in the ability to lead. Without a common language or vocabulary to draw from, all strategy and development is susceptible to misinterpretation and ineffectiveness.

It is important that leaders make sure that there is a common vocabulary used amongst the members of their circle. The vocabulary should not be complicated or used to make others feel inadequate compared to you as a leader; it should be comprehensible and welcoming, not full of jargon. This makes it easier for all individuals to understand messages using the same tone and defined purpose. With a clear vocabulary, if your team, staff, or followers expand beyond what you expected, you will still be effective at communicating strategy, goals, and objectives. The goal with your vocabulary is to make sure it is simple enough to be understood, yet persuasive enough to spark fire in the hearts of your people and have them think about exactly what they can contribute to the overall mission.

Raise the Level of Leadership

Leaders must keep in mind the need to raise the bar on their leadership team. As the number of your followers increases, so should your level of communication rise. As you embrace more responsibility, so should your support team. It is up to you to make sure the awareness and understanding of what needs to elevated is embraced in its entirety.

If there is a lack in communication and clarity about what needs to be done, the following situations happen:

★ Weak execution of strategies due to misunderstood priorities

★ Waste of valuable resources

★ Waste of valuable time to correct and clarify the direction

★ Lack of faith in the presented strategy

★ Lack of understanding of the leadership direction

Business dictionaries state that organizational culture encompasses values and behaviors that "contribute to the unique social and psychological environment of an organization. Culture is the collection of organization's focus, vision, values, norms, systems, symbols, language, assumptions, beliefs, and habits." When changes have to be made from the top to the bottom, a lack of communication and clarity can, and probably will, hinder the growth of the business culture. There could be utter confusion when the key factors that make up a culture become blurred.

Get Rid of THEY and Stick with WE

Any leader is vulnerable to falling victim to the word "THEY." "THEY" signifies a separation amongst the team. The term "WE" should be used as often as possible as when discussing an upcoming or accomplished goal. There will be moments when things get confusing or someone may have dropped the ball on a task. Rather than making it a group issue, leaders within an organization will mistakenly use the term "THEY" to avoid assigning responsibility for the issue(s) at hand. However, true leadership involves taking ownership for making things happen and making things better when the ball has been dropped. Furthermore, using the term "WE" encourages camaraderie and leaves little to no room for pointing fingers. Effective leadership and strategy makes sure that "WE" is embraced on every level of the organization to promote positive progress on all fronts.

As the spearhead of your organization, you should try your best to push the term "WE" throughout the entire group. When a mission has been achieved, the entire organization benefits ("WE" benefit). If something didn't go right, whether it's from the top leadership, middle management, or the interns, "WE" all messed up. There has to be unity in the language for the changes and progress to be made as a whole. When your entire team uses the term "WE" more than the term "THEY," your culture evolves. The strategies you have developed can be implemented, knowing that everyone will be taking responsibility to ensure the plan is properly executed.

Get away from terms like "THEY" that separate valuable people from valuable responsibility. Be effective in your examples when showing your followers and your team the difference between unified vocabulary and destructive ideology. You, as the global leader that you are, have a responsibility in this world. That responsibility is to bring humanity together, starting with those who are in your circle and who follow you.

www.ingramcontent.com/pod-product-compliance
Lightning Source LLC
LaVergne TN
LVHW051556070426
835507LV00021B/2609